THE EDGE OF THE ABYSS

The Edge of the Abyss

By Alfred Noyes

Delicta majorum immeritus lues,
Romane, donec templa refeceris
aedesque labentes deorum.

NEW YORK

E. P. Dutton and Company, Inc.

1942

S. A. JACOBS, THE GOLDEN EAGLE PRESS
MOUNT VERNON, N. Y.

Dedicated to my friend

DUNCAN CAMPBELL SCOTT

*first of contemporary Canadian poets
in whom the great tradition is reconciled
with all that is best of our own day*

PREFACE

It is commonly said that the world conflict is "not a war but a revolution"; and, apparently, we are expected to approve of the latter, without asking too many questions. It is a dangerous approval, unless we ask the following questions: *Whose revolution is it? Who began it? Where is it taking us?*

These questions cannot be answered merely by "smearing" those who had not hitherto been clamoring for "revolution," or even by accusing them of "apathy." There are many, probably the majority, whose chief desire was for those very simple forms of happiness and the "good life" which are too often denied to them by more vocal minorities. To these it may have seemed that the world — if it had not been for the revolutionaries of both the Right and the Left — was, on the whole, progressing. It would be disastrous if we found that the idea behind both the "war" and the "revolution" were in effect the same; and that the very thing the United Nations had been fighting had been foisted on us under another name.

This book, however, is a plea for certain profound changes in the heart and mind of the modern world, changes absolutely necessary if we are to "win the

7

peace." To these changes the victory of the four free-
doms as outlined in the Atlantic Charter is an essential
preliminary. No analysis should be allowed to obscure
that postulate.

I wish further to say that if, in attacking what seems
to me to be radically wrong in our own modern neo-
pagan world, I have spoken very freely and openly, I
can only hope that it may strengthen the indictment
of the criminal aggressors in whom those evils came to
a head. In the matter of literature, some of the questions
raised may seem almost irrelevant at a time like this;
but, if it be true that there is something wrong in our
management of that great instrument of thought —
and I honestly feel that there is — it is far from being
irrelevant. Finally, if I have hurt the susceptibilities of
any whom I have misunderstood, in the following
pages, I hope that they will attribute it only to my own
intense feeling. We are perhaps all of us to blame to a
certain extent for the present confusion of the values
which were once our inestimable heritage. My book
has been written under difficulties; but it does represent an honest conviction, developed during a long
period of years; and I can only say, in conclusion, that
if I seem to have spoken too strongly here and there, I
have also kept back much that might have been brought
forward in support of my thesis, out of a desire to say
no more than was necessary to give "chapter and
verse."

Preface

The English-speaking peoples hitherto have always been able to distinguish between love of country, and State-worship.

The hope of the world is with the English-speaking peoples; and it is to them today that the ancient poet's adjuration may be addressed:

> *Delicta majorum immeritus lues,*
> *Romane, donec templa refeceris*
> *aedesque labentes deorum.*

The sins of thy forefathers, O Roman, thou, though guiltless, shalt expiate, till thou restorest the crumbling temples of the gods.

ACKNOWLEDGMENTS

THE Canadian edition of this book was published by Mount Allison University, in Sackville, New Brunswick, Canada, where a considerable part of it was given recently on the Josiah Wood Lecture Foundation. This course, as Sir James Irvine pointed out, corresponds closely to the Gifford Lectureship at the Scottish Universities, which, in its original intention, envisaged the recovery of the *Civitas Dei*. My thanks are due to the Board of Regents for so graciously facilitating the arrangements for this enlarged American edition.

My thanks are also due for permission to reprint excerpts from the following:

G. K. Chesterton, "Wife of Flanders" from *The Collected Poems of G. K. Chesterton*, copyright 1911 by Dodd, Mead & Co., Inc.

Winston S. Churchill, *Great Contemporaries*, courtesy of G. P. Putnam's Sons.

Georges Clemenceau, *Grandeur and Misery of Victory*, translated from the French by F. M. Atkinson, Harcourt, Brace & Co., Inc.

Dr. Charles Gore, *The Reconstruction of Belief*, Charles Scribner's Sons.

Acknowledgments

Walter Lippmann, Phi Beta Kappa Address delivered
before the American Association for the Advance-
ment of Science, December 29, 1940.

Louis Untermeyer, *From Another World: The Autobiography of Louis Untermeyer*, Harcourt, Brace
& Co., Inc., 1939.

A. N.

THE EDGE OF THE ABYSS

CHAPTER I

ABOUT twenty-four years ago, after the apparent
conclusion of the World War of 1914-1918, I wrote
an article for *The Saturday Evening Post* on what I then
believed to be the signs of approaching disaster to our
civilization. This article evoked a host of letters agree-
ing with it, letters couched sometimes in terms of
passionate conviction, which left no doubt as to the
sincerity and deep concern of their writers, all of whom
represented the ordinary man with a sense of right and
wrong. They included soldiers, sailors, engineers,
educators, men of science, but no politicians.

The course of events since that day has so completely
confirmed what those writers, and the article, had felt
to be in the air, that it may justify a quotation from the
opening paragraph.

A few years ago [it began] ... this article would have
seemed fantastic to the majority of level-headed men
and women. Today it is the expression of a constant
thought that troubles all of us. It is the most level-headed
members of the community who are most anxious. Only
the irresponsible and thoughtless are unconscious of a
vast peril to that slow growth of the ages which we call
our civilization. Practical men, with their feet planted
solidly on the earth, are staring into the future as into an
immeasurable darkness; and they are not sure whether

there is solid ground in front of them or whether the next few steps may bring them to the brink of a precipice.

Since that was written, the brink has been reached and, by general acknowledgment, it is the edge of a sheer abyss.

The title of this brief book, then, represents a grim reality, a peril infinitely more grave than those "perils to civilization" and "threats to democracy" which the Anglo-Saxon political world has discovered, all too tardily, in the last decade or two. The War, with all its horror, the programmes of the totalitarian despotisms, with all their wickedness, are hardly more than symptomatic eruptions, evidence of something so profoundly wrong with modern civilization that, unless the War brings the world to its senses, and quickly, the human race may as well abandon itself to the final catastrophe. A certain height, with glimpses of a height beyond, it did once reach; but there has never been any ground, and there is less ground than ever today, for assuming that "progress" (with merely temporary setbacks of universal massacre) would be automatic and indefinite.

Every natural and historical analogy suggests the opposite. It was perfectly clear, at one time, that the future direction of human progress must be along the road of spiritual values and the development of character, or what a great poet called "soul-making." We were not going to improve very much on the sinews of the tiger or the eye of the eagle. A fine and lucid American thinker, Fiske, pointed out that while — on the physical side — evolution had not carried us beyond various other branches of the animal world, the gulf on the mental and spiritual side was almost immeasurable; and that this now seemed to be the true line of our progress towards any real betterment of the race, and the heights beyond. But this line, this road, in recent decades, has not only been lost, it has been cynically erased from the map of the universe; and the mechanistic developments of our time have not atoned for the loss. They have simply increased its penalties. When Thoreau thanked God that man had not yet learned to fly, he had no foresight of the desecrated hearths and altars of humanity, but he was wiser than he knew.

We must look deeper than the political catastrophes of the modern world; deeper than the disasters of a mechanized industrialism in which starvation and over-production can exist side by side, if we would find the real cause of the contemporary tragedy. Tragedy, beyond all tragedy, it is admitted to be, wherever individual men and women speak their real thoughts to one another — that mankind, with the sun in heaven, the wisdom of the ages in its libraries, the resources of science at its feet, and so many means of simple happiness within its grasp, should be living in a State-created hell of hatred and destruction. The cause of this tragedy is neither political nor economic. It is that the race has been induced to forget its true end, through which happiness (or Carlyle's "blessedness") alone can come. There is hardly a man, among all the millions now at the death grapple, who would not think himself almost in Paradise, if he could be vouchsafed that very simple blessing, the opportunity of making and possessing in security what Burns called "the happy fire-side clime, for weans and wife." But of this individual happiness, which today could certainly be procured for the vast majority of the race, the totalitarian State — that monstrous Juggernaut — takes no cognizance, though the only reason for the existence of organized states is that they should serve each and every individual in precisely that respect. The cost of a single year of this war could have assured that end to every man living. But the State is no longer the instrument of that end. Over a large part of the world it has become the Master, and more than the Master, a blood-stained Idol, a false god, dictating (for its "ambiguous" oracles know how to speak through its mouth) to the helpless millions at its feet. It has induced them to forget the real values of the individual soul, and the true end of the State, which is to subserve those values.

Even in the political world, the present conflict is at last seen to be something more than political or economic — though it is doubtful whether any of the

The Edge of the Abyss

political leaders yet realize the profound truth that it is a "battle for the possession of the human soul" — and that the real victory can only be won in the realms of thought, by a profound change in that realm throughout the world. In fact, the "democracies" are in danger of being forced into totalitarianism to fight totalitarianism; and to cast out devils with the aid of Beelzebub. But we do begin to find strange phrases about "good" and "evil," taking the place of the usual verbal counters of political rhetoric. We begin to hear of "Christian principles," though all too often in circumstances which, as Mr. Hoover said recently, make the very phrase sound like a Gargantuan joke. This does not mean that the appeal to "Christian principles" is wrong; but it does mean that those who make it are in a dilemma. Sometimes (in the agnostic, pagan, cynical, "amoral" atmosphere of modern politics) it sounds like the cry of men who are being carried along by a swirling flood, through whirlpool after whirlpool, to the edge of Niagara. The great mass of people in the English-speaking world have never lost their sense of certain values which the arbiters of our intellectual fashions have for so long tried to sneer out of existence; and it is here, among the plain people, the "constituents," who have been temporarily rendered almost helpless by the bureaucratic machinery, that the hope, the only hope of the world now abides. Theoretically "free," they are everywhere in chains; but the chains still depend on a certain relationship between the higher and the lower. There are still millions of good, simple, kindly individuals in the world.

> Truthful, trustful, looking upward to the practised
> hustings-liar.
> So the higher wields the lower, while the lower is
> the higher.

Moreover, the falsities of the modern world of "high politics" have brought about a situation which, with an almost farcical simplicity, is daily demonstrating them to be false. In its simplest form, here is one side of the picture. We are told that the Government X is a government of criminals, murderers, and utterly untrustworthy liars who will say anything and do anything to obtain their ends. Unforeseen circumstances then bring us into co-operation with this government; but, before we lend this government of utterly untrustworthy criminals our full co-operation we naïvely ask their liar-in-chief to make us a pretty little nursery promise that he will not cease to co-operate with us before we have achieved our own highly moral and Christian ends. We explain that we are co-operating reluctantly because he is a murderer and a liar, whose first principle is to break his word whenever he finds it convenient; and we then, like infants in pinafores, ask him please to give us his "promise," to which we

The Edge of the Abyss

apparently attach precisely the value which we openly say it does not and cannot possess.

But that is only a picture of a single incident, and the question has universal bearings. It has been asked a thousand times in recent months. In its usual and most elementary form it was: *How can we be sure that any treaty or contract will be kept by our enemies when this war is over? How can we be sure that any agreement will be kept for a single hour if it appears advantageous to them to break it?*

But the question has far wider and deeper aspects than that. It can be asked in a far more comprehensive form: *How can we build a stable world again, or find any security for our children, or believe in any of the higher values that make life worth living, when the very foundations of all real belief have been shattered or sneered out of existence, in the intellectual and spiritual collapse of Western civilization? What right, what possible right, have even those politically conservative journals which, in their neo-pagan literary columns have continually tried to demonstrate their pseudo-intellectual superiority to all the "bourgeois virtues," and especially to that "bourgeois virtue, truth"—what possible right have they to ask that the "bourgeois virtues" should now be smugly re-enthroned, for their own benefit, in international affairs?*

The Edge of the Abyss

Today [as Mr. Christopher Dawson wrote recently]
England and the whole world are passing through a terrible crisis. We are fighting not merely against external
enemies, but against powerful forces that threaten the
very existence of our culture. The present conflict is not
just a material struggle for markets and territory. It is a
battle for the possession of the human soul. Western civilization is threatened not by the blind violence of the
barbarian, but by a far more sinister power which strikes
directly at the moral foundations of our civilization and
releases the forces of destruction which have been held
in check by a thousand years of Christian culture.

And this is not a sudden eruption. The forces of
destruction have been at work, within our borders,
over a long period. For more than half a century, in
the literature of the pseudo-intellectuals and neo-
pagans all over the world, the sapping and mining has
been carried on, with a curiously malicious ardor of
concentration, confusing all the lines of right and
wrong, and all the loyalties of mankind.

CHAPTER II

THERE must be an ironic twist in the grim smile of the recording angel, when those who have displayed nothing but irony towards all the common loyalties in the past, are now forced to bleat for morals and Christian principles. Forced, because faced with this elementary but urgent practical question: *What promise can we trust, what firm agreement can ever be made again, in a world where millions upon millions have been educated to believe that, if it seems in their interest to violate it, no pact or pledge, however solemnly drawn up, need be regarded by "realistic" minds, or "cold statesmanship," as more than a "scrap of paper," even though its violation involve the murder by night of sleeping and innocent millions?*

But that again is only a particular instance of the far deeper, universal question: How can we re-establish a firm faith in the imperatives of the conscience and the absolute distinction between right and wrong, good and evil, when conscience itself has been explained away by the exponents of modern materialism, and the very ground for the absolute distinction between right and wrong, which was once derived from the eternal nature of the Supreme Being or God, has been cut away from under our feet, or ridiculed by incompetent

23

thinkers as a survival of primitive taboos. The relativities of the modern casuist are of no use to us here. To play with relativities when you are choosing life or death for your children is to be lost. There is no relativity about the murder of the innocent. The ground of this distinction between good and evil here is *absolute;* the imperatives of the conscience absolute; but an immense part of the modern world, for quite inadequate reasons and under the guidance of incompetent pseudo-intellectuals, has lost its religion, and plunged all those absolute distinctions and imperatives into a new chaos. I am not speaking merely of formal religion; though, without form, chaos again returns. I am speaking of the faith that supported statesmen like Lincoln, or revolutionists like Mazzini. This has ceased to exist among the political leaders of Europe today; and the evil political conditions, as a direct consequence, almost defy description. The following words were written more than ten years ago by Mr. Churchill, in an article on Clemenceau; written, it is to be noted, not of the dregs of the underworld, but of men who were supposed to be guiding the destinies of a great nation.

> *The life of the French Chamber, hectic, fierce, poisonous, flowed through a succession of scandals and swindles, of exposures, of perjuries, forgeries and murders, of plottings and intriguings, of personal ambitions and revenges, of crooking and double-crossing, which find their modern parallel only in the underworld of Chicago. But here*

they were presented upon the lime-lit stage of the most famous of the nations before an audience of all the world. The actors were men of the highest ability; men of learning and eloquence; men of repute and power; men who proclaimed the noblest sentiments; who lived in the public eye; men who directed armies, diplomacy and finance. It was a terrible society, grimly polished, loaded with explosives, trellised with live electric wires.

To one word in that description we may take exception, the word "*highest*." It is a confusion of values, which perfectly illustrates the general confusion. But it may be added that the rest of Mr. Churchill's description was undoubtedly true, and that it has terrible implications, when one remembers how little the true conditions were realized at that time by the confiding people of the British Commonwealth of Nations. The aims and ideals of the vast majority of individuals comprising that Commonwealth have — on the whole — been as good and true as any known to history. Yet its destinies were attached, in the highest-sounding public language, to this poisonous gang of criminals and murderers; and not one man in any ten million citizens of the Commonwealth had the faintest idea of the true state of affairs. Kipling, the poet of the Empire, undoubtedly expressed a sincere belief, when he spoke of France as "first to follow truth, and last to leave old truths behind." But even there we may detect an attempt to eat our cake and have it; and the words of

The Edge of the Abyss

Swinburne seem to come nearer to the cold facts as Mr. Churchill gave them.

> *France, what of the night?*
>   Night is the prostitute's noon,
>   Kissed and drugged till she swoon,
> Spat upon, trod upon, whored,
> Blood-red, with rose-garlands dight,
>   Round me reels in the dance
> Death, my Savior, my Lord,
>   Crowned. There is no more France.

The description of the men who, over a long period of time, controlled the destinies of France, was not a poetical one. It was that of a statesman, Mr. Churchill, who had to have practical dealings with them, and therefore must have known what he was talking about. It is no news that there are criminals, forgers, and murderers in the underworld. But to many of those simple folk who took the word "civilization" at its face value and still retained a real sense of right and wrong it must be somewhat startling to find that, over a long period of time, criminals, forgers, and murderers occupied high government positions, among our allies, as well as among our enemies; and that, among the controllers of the destinies of Europe, it must long have been the rule rather than the exception to meet criminals and murderers as eminent members of their own profession.

26

CHAPTER III

AN illustration of how an entirely well-meaning political organization in England was rendered completely
unmoral by the prevalent confusion of thought was
offered in 1938, when a section of the British Labour
Party, rightly or wrongly, sent a protest to Moscow
against those strange trials in which large numbers of
prisoners appeared to welcome the death sentence
rather than attempt to defend themselves, or to endure
what would happen to them in secret if they did
attempt publicly to defend themselves. According to
the most responsible journals of the time, it was a
scene to freeze the blood. The most ghastly hints of
what had been done privately to the victims by the
official representatives of one of the greatest powers
in the world were printed in journals of the highest
standing, including the London *Times*, and the chief
newspapers of almost every other nation. Whether
those hints were true or not, is a question that does not
affect in the slightest degree the appalling state of
affairs which made the hints possible. That the hints
could be made at all; that any part of Europe could be
in such a condition that such hints were ever conceiv-
able, would be bad enough. But we are concerned now

27

with something nearer home, and something completely verifiable. A political organization in England, as I said, addressed a protest against those horrors, which it denounced in the strongest terms. It described those "legal murders" and "baths of blood" as a reversion to "bestiality." It used the word "bestiality"; and then, in the very next paragraph, it illustrated the complete moral confusion of our time by calling on the very men whom it had just denounced as "bestial" to abandon the methods of "bestiality" on the ground that these methods were bad "propaganda" for their common cause — and it actually told the alleged exponents of the very "bestiality" against which it protested that, if they would only cease to murder, they might be accepted as the foremost leaders of the democratic movement throughout the world.

Nobody supposes for a moment that the individual members of any party in any English-speaking country desired to be led by men whom that party had itself described as having committed fiendish and bestial crimes. But this is precisely what this protest asserted, in cold print. It was the offer openly made to the beasts. Blood may be washed off; but the cold print remains. If the charges are now withdrawn what are we to think of the appalling wickedness that made them?

The party in question was not alone in the dilemma which, through a radical flaw in modern political

28

thought, is constantly dragging the entire world towards disaster. We have seen it again and again; in the conduct of all parties that for a political, or an economic, or a national end, or for conveniences of trade, have agreed to recognize the powerful criminal and forget the crime. (Though each separate individual in those parties would quite possibly have found the ethical barrier unbreakable.) The flaw in modern political thought is this: the necessary subordination of the individual to the State (or indeed to any organization, society or club, of which he is a member) has led us all, in various degrees, to a tragic fallacy about the nature of that relationship.

We hear a great deal about the value of the individual in democratic countries; but that value, once the central value of Christendom, has been made to subserve the political and bureaucratic machines. In almost everything that concerns human beings most — their thoughts, their affections, and the lives of those dear to them — the individual human being of average intelligence and character is necessarily far ahead of any man-made organization, no matter how large or mechanically powerful. Mentally and morally, the individual human being is bound to be in advance of those larger but far more crudely organized bodies — or abstractions — which we loosely personify as nations, states, bureaucracies, or even political parties. It is exactly true that committees have no conscience.

The Edge of the Abyss

It is just as impossible for them to have a common conscience as it is for them to have a child in common, and to feel towards that child exactly as the individual mother feels. It was not Shakespeare, but one of his characters — and not one of the wisest — who suggested that a complete human personality might represent only a blind finger or great toe of either a mob or a state. The analogy is utterly false. All human beings have far too much in common to admit of distinctions so extreme. If we must use an organic figure, the infinitely truer sentence may be recalled: *"I am the Vine; ye are the branches."* There is the perfect image of communion and fellowship, human and divine. But man-made institutions are not, and cannot be, organized in such a way that the higher qualities of the individual are imparted to them. The State, for instance, cannot have a highly organized nervous system of its own, exquisitely sensitive to the feelings of its neighbors, or comparable with the organization of nerves and brain in the individual. The State can imitate those infinitely finer organizations by its crude apparatus of cables, telephone exchanges, railroads, and wireless telegraphy. We may talk loosely of the nerve centers of a city or a state; but, even so, it remains a loosely knit monster, capable of mechanically destroying its creators or trampling them into a quagmire of blood, if they try to let it do their thinking for them.

The Edge of the Abyss

What nation yet has risen above brute nature?
  Though Love illumed each separate striving mind,
Like some half-blind, half-formed primeval creature
  The State still crawled ten thousand years behind.

There were attempts in the political world between
1918 and 1938 to reassert those values in which the
humblest individual, and indeed *every* individual,
really does transcend the machine; but they were
nearly all stultified by the fact that it was to the machine that they made their appeal; to the League, for
instance, and its illusory command of collective and
subhuman machinery for controlling other machines;
not to the League as a means of communication between the minds and hearts of men. We appealed to
the false and subhuman personifications of State and
Party; and we might as well have tried to avoid disaster
on a railway line by addressing protests to the steam
engine. Thought is still powerful, but its only appeal
is to the separate individual. It can be spread very
widely, if it is sincere, at a smaller cost than universal
disaster. It is all very well to ask "why England slept"
while the world was moving towards the disaster. I cannot say what that abstraction — the State — was doing;
but I know that the millions of individuals who make
up England were not asleep. They simply did not
possess the information which ought to have been imparted to them, and to the entire world. It is not, and

cannot be right; it is an insult to the intelligence and
spirit of mankind to suggest that information of such
dire importance to the entire race must be religiously
confined to a few officials, while everyone else must
be regarded as in a state of arrested development, or
adolescent tutelage, not to be trusted with the dangerous facts, or that it is the duty of the countless millions,
whose lives and all that is dear to them are at stake,
merely to open their mouths and shut their eyes and
see what the professional politicians, dictators, or
demagogues, will give them.

That fine New England thinker, Thoreau, sometimes appeared to forget the second half of the motto:
"All for each, and each for all," which is the perfect
expression of the democratic ideal, and includes duties
as well as rights. But he uttered a profound truth when
he said that the injustice of the State towards a single
individual life (the life of a Negro slave) was a general
disaster.

> The effect of a good government [he wrote] is to make
> life more valuable — of a bad government to make it less
> valuable. We can afford that railroad and all merely ma-
> terial stock should depreciate, for loss only compels us to
> live more simply and economically; but suppose the value
> of life itself should be depreciated. Every man in New
> England capable of the sentiment of patriotism must
> have lived the last three weeks with the sense of having
> suffered a vast, indefinite loss. I had never respected this

government, but I had foolishly thought that I might manage to live here, attending to my private affairs, and forget it. For my part, my old and worthiest pursuits have lost I cannot say how much of their attraction, and I feel that my investment in life here is worth many per cent less since Massachusetts last deliberately and forcibly restored an innocent man, Anthony Burns, to slavery. I dwelt before in the illusion that my life passed somewhere only *between* heaven and hell, but now I cannot persuade myself that I do not dwell wholly within hell.... Life itself being worthless, all things with it, that feed it, are worthless. .... I am surprised to see men going about their business as if nothing had happened; that the man whom I just met on horseback should be so earnest to overtake his newly bought cows running away — since all property is insecure, and if they do not run away again, they may be taken away from him when he gets them.... The remembrance of the baseness of politicians spoils my walks. My thoughts are murder to the State.

Again:

I wish my criticizer to consider that, whatever the human law may be, neither an individual nor a nation can ever commit the least act of injustice against the obscurest individual without having to pay the penalty for it.

And again:

There will never be a really free and enlightened State until the State comes to recognize the individual as a

*higher and independent power, from which all its own
power and authority are derived.*

This is the lost key to the whole problem of modern
government; but it depends, itself, on another lost
truth — from which all the value of the individual is
derived. It was expressed by another New England
thinker, Henry Ward Beecher.

> Christ did not die for laws or governments.
> He did not die to build a nation up.
> He died for men, the separate souls of men.

The crux of the whole Christian philosophy is that
the Supreme Being (the Power above the State, so
violently denied by the totalitarians) does actually
meet and communicate with the spirit of man, in his
inner personal life; or, as St. Augustine put it, "God
stoops to man that man may rise to God." It is the
eternal Vine which gives the life and value to the
branches; and it is a value that belongs only to the
personal life, which is individual; to each living separate
soul, not to institutions, or committees, or clubs, or
cabinets, or governments, or states.

The State was made for man, not man for the State.
The State may be immensely useful to the individual
men who have made it; but it did not make men, and
it may be harmful to them. No philosopher, even in
this mad world, has yet maintained that the State was

34

The Edge of the Abyss

destined for Eternal Life. But the greatest of all philosophies has maintained, rightly or wrongly, for two
thousand years, that the individual human soul was
created for that high destiny; that the value of the
individual human soul is immeasurable because it is
capable of rising to communion with God and "enjoy-
ing Him for ever." This is the proposition upon which
Christendom was founded, and it is the only proposition upon which we can guard the otherwise quite
arbitrary claims of the great charters of human freedom. There is something appallingly wrong, something
tragically wrong, with a world in which hundreds
of millions of those individuals whom Christ died to
save, are hurled helplessly into bloodshed by half
a dozen men whose plans and motives have been completely hidden from all but perhaps another half dozen;
so that entire nations, which in their general level of
individual character and intelligence — not to speak of
their outstanding individuals, a Beethoven, a Pasteur,
a Shakespeare, a Galileo — have far surpassed the level
of the half dozen manipulators of the political machinery, suddenly find themselves helplessly slaughter-
ing one another.

CHAPTER IV

THE World War of 1914-1918 immensely increased
the size and number of the bureaucratic departments,
and riveted a governmental grip upon our lives which
was certainly quite unprecedented in English history.
Imposed upon us to meet a despotically controlled
enemy, those methods were described — perhaps rightly — as necessary to the prosecution of the war, and
as merely "temporary." But the bureaucratic grip has
never been loosened. Lord Hewart, the late Lord Chief
Justice of England, made protest after protest against it,
but entirely in vain. During the last twenty-five years
it has increased to such an extent that we seem to be
nearing a time when we shall be required to fill out
government forms stating how much air we breathe.
Freedom of movement from one part of the world to
another has been unbelievably restricted. The most
unoffending private citizens are harassed by all kinds
of forms, passports, visas, and armies of officials (all
of whom have to be paid by the taxpayers), while the
political figures who were described by Mr. Churchill
as criminals and murderers, have never failed to find
all the doors smoothly opening for them. Among all
the millions of private citizens who are harassed and
delayed by restrictions imposed by the machine
(which is entirely at the service of the very people

who ought not only to be restricted but incarcerated),
there may be a small number of persons whom it would
be desirable to keep under observation by the State.
But these are certainly cunning enough to slip through
all the clumsy frontier regulations. It is only the criminal department that can cope with these. The wasteful-
ness of employing a highly paid legion of officials to
examine or bully all the millions of unoffending private
citizens individually — the very cost of the printing
of the innumerable forms — would be a monument of
stupidity, if it were not all too logically consistent with
the increasingly despotic control of the individual by
the bureaucratic machine. That is the real point, and
the smoothing and deepening of the channels from the
earnings of the taxpayer to the pockets of the entirely unproductive bureaucrats. "Economic recovery"
meant merely that there were larger opportunities for
taxation wherewith to nourish these parasitical growths.
The "cells" grew and multiplied, as in some evil can-
cer, until the private citizen could hardly plant a
kitchen garden or keep a few hens without being
besieged by salaried officials with immense printed
forms asking innumerable questions about the ages
of the hens and the comparative quantities of lettuces
and onions produced in that and previous years.

These forms often threatened absurd penalties of
fines and imprisonment if the questions were not
answered and the officials satisfied. In England, hither-

to, the penalties have not been imposed to any considerable extent, chiefly because our "Village Hampdens" merely grumble and submit. But governments change; and one day these printed threats may be a weapon in the wrong hands. The "growth of the cells" was part of the very policy which Communism set itself to encourage. One of the foremost English judges, not so long ago, in peacetime, declared that some of the bureaucratic interferences with English farmers reminded him of the methods of the Star Chamber.

The vicious circle in which we are moving today is a maelstrom; but it may be illustrated, in simpler fashion, by a minor whirlpool of an earlier date. In the early part of the last century, when the North American Indians were rapidly being dispossessed of their last foothold in their native land by the advance forces of "civilization," the Red Man and the White Man were often at "war." The weapons of the White Man were, in order of destructiveness, whiskey, fraudulent trade, and — where these failed to destroy and dispossess — the rifle bullet. Of the Red Man's weapons, at this very time, Catlin in his *Manners, Customs, and Conditions of the North American Indians*, makes these notable remarks:

> The scalping-knives and tomahawks are of civilized manufacture, made expressly for Indian use, and carried into the Indian country by thousands and tens of thousands, and sold at an enormous price. The scabbards of

the knives and handles for the tomahawks, the Indians construct themselves according to their own taste, and oftentimes ornament them very handsomely. In his rude and unapproached condition, the Indian is a stranger to such weapons as these; and his untutored mind has not been ingenious enough to design or execute anything so savage or destructive as these civilized refinements on Indian barbarity. In his native simplicity, he shapes out his rude hatchet from a piece of stone. The war-club is another civilized refinement, with a blade of steel of eight or ten inches in length and set in a club, studded around and ornamented with some hundreds of brass nails. . . .

The scalping-knife, in a beautiful scabbard [the latter made by the Indian], is a common and cheap butcher knife, manufactured at Sheffield, in England, perhaps, for sixpence; and sold to the poor Indian in these wild regions for a horse. If I should live to get home, and should ever cross the Atlantic with my collection, a curious enigma would be solved for the English people, who may inquire for a scalping-knife, when they find that every one in my collection (and hear also that nearly every one that is to be seen in the Indian country, and the Rocky Mountains, and the Pacific Ocean) bears on its blade the impress of G. R., which they will doubtless understand. The huge two-edged knife [he says of another weapon] was undoubtedly of American manufacture.

It will be noted that here, as in other cases, however, these revolting facts were given as startling news to the men and women of England and America, who were obviously expected to be revolted as individuals. Companies, corporations, governments knew all about them. This is abundantly clear from the context. But, to those ordinary individuals whom, as Lincoln said, God must have loved best because he made so many of them, the facts were offered as the solution of an "enigma."

The enigma is less easily solved, in the complicated circumstances of modern international politics, but it is of precisely the same character. An American scientist, of the highest integrity, and—incidentally—a lover of England and a wholehearted supporter of her cause in the present war, states that, during the South African War, he happened to be in Germany and in close touch with the official American representatives there. These American representatives were disturbed by the fact that weapons from English factories were arriving at Hamburg for reshipment. They suspected that they were being reshipped to the Philippines. Investigation showed, however, that those weapons from English factories were being reshipped to the Boers in South Africa for use against the unhappy English Army, of whom that genuine patriot, Kipling, wrote so innocently:

> Each of 'em doing his country's work, and who's
>   to look after the things.
> Pass the hat for your credit's sake, and pay—pay—pay.

Whatever our view of the South African War may be (and I, for one, am among those who today believe it to have been a blot on our history, for which we have been paying the penalty ever since 1902), the killing of our own youth — "striplings" as Kipling described them — with munitions sent out from our own factories during the war, was a murdering of the innocent by the wicked for profit. If truth is truth, the same process on a far larger scale is recorded by the late United States Ambassador to Berlin, Mr. Dodds. He set it down in his diary, for all the world to read; and, if the public ignores it or passes it by, it will be because the public is "transported smoothly from point to point of its prescribed existence" and is content to forget. But the consequences of that oblivion will be unescapable.

"The arms manufacturers all over the world are the cause of most of the trouble in Europe," wrote the late Mr. Dodds. It is a terrible charge. It involved the shedding of rivers of innocent blood; and I see no reason why the Ambassador should have made it without cause. "Contrary to the treaty between Germany and the United States, American armament manufacturers sold great quantities of arms to Germany for gold. Nor have the English been better," he wrote. "They have themselves violated the Versailles Treaty in selling aircraft and other war materials to Germany." And this at a time when the German Minister of Economics and President of the Reichsbank, in a private conversation, admitted to the Ambassador that "the Hitler party is absolutely committed to war." This, moreover, at the very time at which other official commissions were compassionately or hypocritically concluding that Germany was unable to meet financial obligations that had been previously incurred for the legitimate purposes of peace.

It was in these terrible conditions that, as an American commentator wrote:

> American, British, and French bankers made huge loans to Germany. American, British and French industrialists in turn sold arms, munitions, and bombers to Germany; and the Nazis, having crushed France, are now turning these American, British and French armaments against the British.

The cynicism of it all is criminal. By the private citizens, in most of these countries, if the facts were fully realized they would be regarded as diabolical. The great majority of private citizens, as individuals, have a real sense of right and wrong, and would be honestly repelled by the maneuvers of those who control the machinery, or are able to make use of it for these evil purposes. It is the very superiority of the individual conscience, however, that inhibits individuals from competing on equal terms with those who have none. The liar has always a temporary advantage over the honest man — as Machiavelli pointed out. The honest man is limited in his choice of methods;

while the dishonest, in the common phrase, "may do anything, and stick at nothing." The consciences of corporations are — at best — rudimentary. They have no apparatus for being anything else; and the big municipality which "takes over" the administration of an adjoining village against the will of its inhabitants may be doing by more peaceful means exactly what, in international affairs, is regarded as a ground for general massacre. In the latter case, individual consciences are inhibited by appeals to what is best in them, their sense of duty, their readiness for sacrifice, and even their humility — that decent instinct of self-effacement, of which the unscrupulously self-assertive so constantly take advantage. The power-greedy have always delighted to point out that better men than themselves are not in possession of the information requisite for forming a judgment — information which the power-greedy have themselves withheld. It becomes the duty, therefore, of better men than themselves, in all other walks of life, to "open their mouths and shut their eyes" and see what the controllers of the machine will give them. At its simplest, it is reduced to

> Theirs not to make reply,
> Theirs not to reason why

And that — whatever it may be on the field of battle — is a demand that mankind should surrender its noblest faculty, the faculty that distinguishes man from the brute. In the actual conditions of war, it may be a necessary surrender; but, in dealing with the conditions that lead to war, it is in direct contradiction of the first principles of that true freedom which is based on universal law, not on the secret knowledge of a gang or coterie. Moreover, it is ridiculous to suggest that the hastily acquired "secret information" of such gangs (especially in the conditions of the present day, when political leaders are continually proving themselves to be completely mistaken), can possibly endow such gangs and coteries with wisdom superior to that of far more intelligent and far better informed men in a thousand other and more honest walks of life. When the politicians have been talking like lunatics, I have often heard, in the study of a man of science or the peaceful studio of an artist at work upon a picture, more plain practical sense than the professional politicians could utter in a thousand years.

And this abominable business has become so peculiar a "preserve" that, if any helpless individuals of the nations concerned were to suggest a sweeping replacement of these tenth-rate gangs by entirely fresh blood, there would be an awe-struck gasp of "but whom can we find to take the place of these Titans?" Such is the power of suggestion through the modern means of "publicity," whereby the giant or figurehead is "built up," paragraph by paragraph, out of straws and inanities, the color of his ties, the food he eats, and the size of his boots. The inside of his head is very seldom examined. And when the gang has finished with him, the giant is taken to pieces or deflated as easily as he was built up or blown out. And this can take place in nations where there are scores of thousands of individuals of higher intelligence and better character. We know, perfectly well, that there is not a country pastor in Germany who would not have served her better as a leader than the "bloodthirsty guttersnipe" to whom her destinies were entrusted. *Mein Kampf* is the answer to anyone who thinks that Hitler was a genius — even though a wicked one. *Mein Kampf* is the revelation of a tenth-rate mind, confused, stunted, devoid of any capacity for high thought. It is precisely because millions of obscure individuals can form just opinions on matters of right and wrong that the democratic idea becomes possible. The prayer of the poet,

> Make no more giants, God,
> But elevate the race,

did not imply that the race was morally, spiritually, or intellectually below the level of these bogus giants who are made, not by God, but by the modern "publicity" methods, at the insistence of the gang, the bureaucrats, or the "general staff," and could be replaced tomorrow by the same agencies if necessary.

46

The Edge of the Abyss

If it be true (and by every principle of freedom and the individual conscience, it *is* true) that the best government is that which governs least, then the movement of the political world during the last fifty years has been progressively towards the worst of all possible systems — a state so completely regimented and ruled, that its members (merely because they are transported or "commuted" smoothly from point to point of their prescribed existence) are lulled to sleep and become completely unconscious slaves of a gigantic machine — robots content to forget the very nature of freedom. But the human soul was created for freedom. Its very character, its very nature as a living soul, depends on this distinction from the automatic machine; a distinction which is rapidly becoming the privilege of the very few who, by hook or by crook, obtain control of the switchboard, and thereafter speak and think of their fellow men in the mass as material for industry, or munitions of war. In recent years, as we have seen, these men in control, by the direct witness of leading statesmen and historians, have often been "criminals, forgers, murderers." *Murderers* is a grim word. But — as we have seen — it was the word used of the French Chamber by Mr. Winston Churchill some years before the present war broke out, and at a time when the French were our "allies." It must be remembered that the word "murderers" was no merely abusive generality, applied to the callous spirit of their political or international operations. It referred to actual killings, and the removal or "liquidation" by death of other men who stood in the murderers' way. Mankind has come to the point where wickedness in the upper regions of the political world is accepted with a shrug of the shoulders, as though its exponents lived on another planet where the ten commandments were abrogated and the writ of God no longer ran. There has been no such peril since the race emerged from the jungle; for, though in many former ages of Christendom there were rulers who behaved like devils, the evil was recognized as evil by the faith and *philosophia perennis* of Christendom; and the faith and creed of Christendom, despite all the failures of their human instruments, were recognized as holding the supreme place in the conscience and the soul. Wickedness, then, was the sin of the individual. Today, in the high places of politics, wickedness is part of a totalitarian creed, a totalitarian philosophy, a totalitarian substitute for religion; in which there is no Power above the State; and it is justified by professors as "relative" righteousness.

It is not surprising, therefore, that these conditions should make possible the appalling facts revealed by a United States ambassador in the diary of his sojourn in Berlin. It is not surprising that business firms should be found, as he relates in cold print, supplying both the materials of war and the funds for their purchase to "enemies" of their own country, enemies whom they knew to be preparing for war against their own country; enemies who would then oblige them by increasing the demand for their products at home and among their allies. To keep the masses of men producing things that can be sold, useful or useless, is their problem. There is one sure temporary way of decreasing unemployment, increasing production, and disposing of the product — war. In war, the factory wheels must be kept roaring and the robots sweating, night and day. And to meet the methods adopted by criminals in countries where Freedom is not cherished, the same methods must be adopted by the countries where Freedom *is* cherished. The British Commonwealth of Nations and the United States of America have grown up with an ideal of Freedom, however imperfectly it may have been realized; but, fighting for their lives, they have no choice. Freedom, temporarily, has been sacrificed. The question of its recovery depends entirely on our ability, when the War is over, to reorganize and alter the appalling ethical conditions which brought it about, and to make sure that, in the future, "forgers" and "murderers" shall not be regarded as men of the "highest ability" for positions in which they can either strut upon the lime-lit stage of the world, or control the lives and deaths of innumerable millions whose only desire is for the "good life."

Evidence of the vicious circle in which we are moving accumulates from too many quarters to be set aside. In that curious book, *Ordeal for England*, by Sir Philip Gibbs, who was a member of the Commission of Enquiry into the armaments business, there are many hints as to the ways in which the evidence may be obscured or shelved; but it is enough to read it in connection with the ambassadorial diary mentioned above. For months before December 7th, 1941, there were suggestions in the newspapers that, at any moment, the United States might be at war with Japan. For a long time past, the United States had ostensibly been supporting China in its war with Japan and on every newspaper there had been headlines to show it. For example, *"Society Leaders Eat Chicken to Launch Chinese Aid Drive."*

Alas, poor Leaders! At that very dinner, an American speaker of the highest reputation made this deadly accusation:

> *As a nation, technically, we have stayed neutral, but we know too well that American scrap iron and oil have kept the Japanese war machine going.*

The accusation, I say, is deadly, though it shrinks from its own terrible consequences. "To keep the war-machine going" sounds to sleepy ears, perhaps, little more significant than to keep the wheels of a factory running. At most, the minds of the hearers are fixed on the political inconsistency.

The Edge of the Abyss

The excuse commonly made is that these supplies are sent to prevent an attack elsewhere. But, quite apart from the proven fact that "Danegeld" and blackmail have never been found satisfactory, the argument is unsound. If an enemy is engaged in killing your friend and is dependent upon you for the weapon, it is an odd argument to say that you will lend him the knife if he will promise not to steal one from the house next door. Odd as an argument, ethically it is fantastic. Heard rightly, the statement that the Japanese war-machine was kept going against China by American scrap iron and oil is just as deadly as the statement that England and France helped to build up the war machine of Germany at a time when Germany was unable to pay even her peacetime obligations. The dreadful charge is shot through by the shrieks of the mutilated and the dying; and by the screams of children, cut down, in bomb-shattered cities, or torn to pieces by shrapnel, that most effective form of scrap iron, day after day, month after month, year after year. It is written in blood and fire across all the skies that overarch the shame and disgrace of our boasted civilization.

All the European nations, together with England, have sinned in the same corporate fashion, and against what would certainly have been the judgment of the vast majority of individual consciences in those nations, if they had been in possession of the facts and had been

51

able to express themselves in opposition to the Juggernaut of the political machine.

It is said, sometimes, in justification of the failure of the State in such matters, that it is "difficult for governments to interfere with private business." But it is to be noticed that governments find no difficulty whatever in devising a hundred regulations for the obscurest and most harmless private individual who wishes to keep a cow, or cross a frontier. It is only when the nefarious business is on a scale so huge that it cannot possibly escape governmental observation, and of a kind so hellish that it sickens the hearts and minds of decent men and women, that the bureaucratic machine suddenly becomes impotent and that the food for the very guns that are levelled at their own flesh and blood finds all the gates opening, all the papers in order, and a smooth passage to the chuckling enemy.

Clemenceau, in his book, *Grandeur and Misery of Victory*, speaks of a financial organization known as the "Gefu," which set itself to defeat the restrictions on armaments made by the Versailles Treaty. Herr Scheidemann, in a speech to the Reichstag as long ago as December 16, 1926, "made revelations on the matter," says Clemenceau, "which are conclusive."

There has been a special section in the Ministry of the Reichswehr under the designation S. G. In Moscow this section has worked in conjunction with the Junker agreements. Since 1923 it has paid out sums amounting to about seventy million gold marks yearly.... It is closely connected with the financial organization known as the Gefu. The manager of this organization is a certain Otto zur Leren, who is usually abroad, more especially in Russia. . . . Direct relations exist between the Ministry of the Reichswehr and the Gefu. The task of the Gefu consists in founding an *armament industry abroad*, especially in Russia. The agreements were signed in false names. The officers sent to Russia, and those coming from there, travelled with faked passports. The Gefu was also to establish in Russia gas-shell factories, a well-known Hamburg chemical factory participating in the operation.

So now we know why gas masks became necessary for the millions of honest folk who had never heard of the "Gefu" and who, on the whole, abstain from fraud and do not "fake" passports. These privileges, including the responsibility for the subsequent mass murders, belong to the criminal few; and the criminal few on the top were able to manipulate the machinery as they pleased, and to "liquidate" those who opposed them with the freedom of the gangsters at the other end of the social scale, in the underworld of Chicago. They, too, had their political affiliations. In the political world, it is certainly true that "extremes meet."

None of those people have a tenth of the difficulty in passing from one country to another that is encountered by a country vicar who wishes to spend a holiday in Europe, in peacetime. The "mystery" (for

democratic countries) of the arrival of Hess in England
may partly be explained by the absolute confidence of
such men that, while honest folk would be shot at sight
if they dared to send a birthday greeting to an old
friend in an "enemy country," an exalted manipulator
of the machine might have a secret conversation with
his co-manipulators on the other side, in order to discuss
how many more millions of men they could respec-
tively "afford to lose." Fortunately, with all her faults,
England has not yet come to that pitch of "totalitarianism."

Is it, then, true or untrue that secret cooperation for
criminal ends between Germany and our present ally,
Russia, goes further back than is commonly supposed
or remembered?

A nation with its back to the wall may have no other
choice, perhaps, than that of the English peer who
remarked in New York: "If the Devil himself fights
Germany, he is our ally!" But it must be remembered
that Finland, whose homes were wrecked and children
murdered by what we all described at the time as the
savage midnight attacks of Russia, has an equal right
to say: "If the Devil himself fights Russia, he is our
ally!" If I can be honestly assured that the whole of
the responsible press of the English-speaking world
was wrong about Finland, and that Russia was right,
I am ready to believe it. But I cannot help possessing
a memory; and, in the meantime, those individuals who

so enthusiastically worked for "aid to Finland" — the heroic defence of which, in England and America, only a few short months ago, was compared with that of Thermopylae — are confronted by the fact that the State has no memory.

It had no memory at the end of the last war to "make the world safe for democracy." It will have no memory at the end of this war to "end armaments and save the world from fear"; no memory whatsoever, except on one possibility, which does not and cannot enter into the public declarations or secret calculations of the State machinery. No statement of peace aims can be more than a straw in the wind, or an election promise, unless it implies a radical change of heart and mind, something far deeper than a glib lip service to the relativities of current ethics. If it is to endure, it must come from the shaken depths of the soul, with a new conviction of the eternal truth: "Seek ye first the kingdom of God and His righteousness, and all these things shall be added unto you."

CHAPTER V

THE history of the idea of true freedom, which can
only be achieved in service to the universal law of
right and of God ("whose service is perfect freedom"),
makes it quite clear that the real good of individuals or,
as Whitman called them, "single, separate persons," is
the proper aim of all social organizations. Magna Carta,
Habeas Corpus, the Declaration of Independence,
were all directed to this end; and the appeal was from
the mechanical authority of despotism to the law of
right and eternal Justice, the Law of God, which is
above the State on the one hand, and is enshrined in
the hearts and minds and consciences of the humblest
individuals on the other. This does not absolve the
individual from his duties to the State. He must render
to Caesar what is rightly due to Caesar; but he must
not render to Caesar what is due only to Almighty
God. Nobody — not Hitler himself — has yet suggested
that the State has an immortal soul. Millions still hold
to the faith that this constitutes the worth and dignity
of the individual human being, on which all "rights"
depend. The individual, therefore, must not transfer
to the State those individual rights and privileges
which, as a French writer said, the English-speaking
nations, and particularly the American people, have

so far considered inseparable from individual welfare and indispensable to national prosperity.

That the people is the source of all political power no American will deny; but the question arises whether it will promote its welfare by abdicating rights which are the foundation of this power to an abstract, ideal entity, whose practical activity cannot be exercised otherwise than through the channels of a bureaucratic oligarchy.

The historical records of the two principal nations of continental Europe which, in direct contradiction to Anglo-Saxon principles have so obstinately continued to invest their government with omnipotent and ideal functions, may awake suspicion that, after all, the State is not a divine goddess having direct access to the shrine of wisdom. The State must always turn out to be a number of more or less intelligent human beings sitting in public buildings — generally on upholstered chairs — surrounded by a vast crowd of their own delegates, all working for wages; all liable, like other men, to be wise or foolish, honest or dishonest, conscientious or not. Wherever the delegated power is too great, wherever, under the pretense of protecting the interests of the people, the State is allowed free scope for interference with individual affairs, political and moral disaster ensues. The collected evidence shows that the individual men who are the component units of the "people" lose their dignity and self-respect, that they become mere dummies in the hands of their paternal State. What fearful atrocities and cruelties are then committed on both sides, when the inevitable struggle takes place to recover from the State rights foolishly delegated by the members of the community.

The Edge of the Abyss

Those words are as true today as when they were written, in 1898. It is the individual members of the people who, as Clemenceau said in 1929, "will have to pay for the abdication of conscience in the State; and they will pay dearly for it."

> The drama of the peace begins. [said that grand old representative of the true France] The German lies have not aroused so much as the slightest protest from the Allied Governments, who are anxious above all things to re-establish their pre-war relations with German industry. . . .
>
> Incredible, yet true! It is Germany, guilty of the greatest crime in the history of Europe, a crime premeditated, prepared and carried out in broad daylight, who presents herself vanquished at the tribunal of Europe and the civilized world, no longer to give an account but to demand one. A lie sets her free. A lie puts us in the dock. . . .

Better by far that there had been no whisper of "material reparations," a phrase that sounds contemptible over the graves of those twenty million dead; better by far that the allied nations had formed themselves into a solemn assize and pronounced judgment on those responsible for the crime against humanity. To do this, we are told, would be "to make martyrs of them," a statement which, curiously enough, is only made about the high and mighty, the lords and masters of the State. The State has no compunction whatsoever in "making a martyr" of any minor gangster that it can catch. We are told that, in any case, it would be impossible to bring the guilt home to the greater gangsters; and that no competent or valid court could be set up. Can Americans and Englishmen presume, we are asked rhetorically, to set themselves up as the supreme judges? The answer to this is that the State has no right to send scores of thousands of our own children to death, or to kill scores of thousands of our neighbors, if the State is not competent to judge the issue. We know that certain diabolical orders were given in the last war. The infamous speech of the German Chancellor, admitting their wrongdoing, is on record; and it was wrongdoing that involved the death of millions. The infamous speech of the Kaiser is on record: "Your duty is to fire on your father and mother if such is my command." The ten commandments are also on record. Even at this atrocious period in human history, they can still be examined by the curious. If any nation had chosen to make a martyr of so "abject a rag of imperialism" as the maker of that speech, it would not have been difficult, in peacetime, with all the modern means of publicity which are so eagerly used for baser purposes, to enlighten the public opinion of that nation, for once in a way, by a little truth-telling. Let such sayings of their own leaders be blared at them, night and day, for a quarter of a century by a thousand wireless stations. Let the sayings be inscribed on the martyrs' monument, and let the monument be as massive as the Pyramids. Let the sayings be illuminated at night, so that all who see them and remember how they accepted them, bow their heads in shame. It would be more effective and less costly than the final world-crime of universal massacre which will certainly be committed and seal the doom of civilization, unless the human race undergoes a profound change of heart. The rebuilding of trade will not do it. But the State has, at least, one all too common human attribute. It is the perfect hypocrite. It tells the rank and file that they are the police force of freedom and civilization; and, when they have cornered the murderer, he is allowed to retire on a handsome fortune, while thousands of the rank and file, blinded, maimed, mutilated, coughing the gas out of their lungs, beg their bread in the streets, or beat their heads against the walls of lunatic asylums. We do know that thousands of innocent folk were slaughtered in Belgium in 1916. We know that the orders were given and we know who gave them. We know that the German Chancellor himself described it as "wrongdoing," and that he openly justified it by what he supposed to be material advantages to Germany. We know that these killings by every law of God and man were nothing but brutal criminal murders on a vast scale; and, when the Allied Governments had it in their power to make this clear to the whole world and for all time, they deliberately concentrated on trade revival and impossible financial reparations which were to be extorted, not from those responsible, but from their helpless puppets, the blinded and deluded people of Germany. We had court-martialled and shot the worn-out sentry who went to sleep at his post, volunteer though he may have been in the cause of Liberty. We had court-martialled and shot our own heroic men whose nerves, after years of superb endurance in the blood and filth of the trenches, had momentarily given way. "And so," says one English writer, now in the British House of Commons, "they shot for cowardice my friend X — who was the bravest man I ever knew." But the men who had brought this horror on the world and had given the orders for its perpetration became owners of large country estates, or high functionaries of the new State machinery which was at once set to work to prepare the new crime of 1939, involving in sorrow and ruin, despair and death, millions upon millions of helpless human beings.

We ourselves continually say, with a note of despair, "What can we do with eighty million Germans, even though they are defeated?" The answer is as clear as daylight. But we constantly evade it.

In 1918, the only right course was to have displayed the utmost generosity towards the great mass of the German people who had been so grievously misled and to have recognized that *this could only be done*

The Edge of the Abyss

by simultaneously insisting on the just penalty for those few — a hundred and fifty, perhaps, at most — who had been responsible for one of the blackest crimes in human history.

But if this were indeed "impossible," financial reparations were, in the sight of high heaven, as impossible as to the "Wife of Flanders."

> Must I for more than carnage call you claimant,
>   Paying you a penny for each son you slay?
> Man, the whole globe in gold were no repayment
>   For what you have lost! and how shall I repay?
>
> How shall I pay for one poor graven steeple
>   Whereon you shattered what you shall not know?
> How shall I pay you, miserable people?
>   How shall I pay you everything you owe?

"Restoration of trade" was not the answer; and, if none were to be more responsible than another for the crime, it had been better that all the nations concerned had gone down on their knees and prayed to Almighty God for forgiveness for the unspeakable sin that they had all committed in common. But before the "sweet familiar sickly stench of the dead" (as one war correspondent called it) had vanished from the torn fields of Europe, the politicians were talking in terms of trade and money. It was a spectacle to draw down the wrath of God upon the whole conception of the modern

The Edge of the Abyss

State in Europe; and perhaps it has indeed drawn it down. Ten years ago Clemenceau foresaw it, in that bitterly ironic passage of almost inspired prophecy:

> I pause on the threshold of the terrible moment when the last great struggle will be entered upon. Who then shall decide the fate of historic France? To what catastrophes may this complete and universal confusion be leading us? It seems at the moment impossible to foresee. The abyss is there, yawning wide, too deep for sounding.
>
> Doubtless the conscience of mankind is a social fact which cannot be abolished at the will of scoundrels. But it has eternity before it, and I have but a day....

CHAPTER VI

AT this stage, a further quotation may be made from the article which I wrote for *The Saturday Evening Post* in 1918. It curiously anticipates the passage already quoted from Mr. Churchill, in which he described the life of the French Chamber as "flowing through a succession of scandals and swindles, of exposures, of perjuries, forgeries and murders . . . which find their modern parallel only in the underworld of Chicago," and so on.

In my article, published some fifteen years earlier, I had written almost exactly the same thing, using almost the same phrases. The "polished" surface of the criminals was a feature in both passages.

The war [I wrote of the World War of 1914-1918] has shown us the complete moral rottenness of two great European empires. It has shown us men of culture, statesmen, diplomats, lying and plotting murder. It has shown us ambassadors, apparently polished gentlemen, turned out by the best tailors, advising their governments to sink the ships of the friendly countries to which they were accredited, *without leaving traces of the human beings aboard those ships.* There is not a crime which devils might be supposed to whisper hoarsely to one another in the darkest regions of hell that these representatives of civilization have not embraced as a virtue.

These charges are based on known and verifiable facts. The passage in italics (the italics have been added), for instance, is a known and verifiable fact. And these charges, with Mr. Churchill's charges, cover the governments of three great European empires. To these we may add the unspeakable crimes committed by successive governments in Russia, and described by the British Labour Party as "bestial." To these we may add the "dagger of the assassin," as wielded by Italy, and described by President Roosevelt in one of the most damning indictments ever delivered by the head of a non-belligerent power. Thus, without reckoning the millions murdered in the East by Japan, we have by far the greater part of "civilization" under criminal control.

A contributory cause was our own failure in 1918 to mark "crime" as "crime." As I wrote in 1918, we had become so familiar with this international wickedness of killing innocent people wholesale that we ceased to realize its utter horror.

The Bryce Report on the ghastly deeds that had been perpetrated faded out of our memories as though it had been a childish nightmare, or a fantastic tale of something that had happened on another planet. The twenty million dead were shovelled out of sight and their tragic memories were disguised or turned to prettiness and favor as "Flanders' poppies." But it was our civilization that had drunk of poppy and mandragora and drugged itself into oblivion of the most appalling crime in the history of mankind.

> The Peace Conference [I wrote] is becoming more and more political in its nature, more and more concerned with technical details. Something more than this is absolutely necessary if we are to make the world safe not only for democracy but for the human soul.

About the same time, in a long letter to the London *Times,* which was quoted by Mr. Healy in the House of Commons, I ventured to prophesy that if, in our haste for material reconstruction, we omitted to bring the crime home to the criminal, or criminals, however highly placed, there would be a growth of cynicism throughout the world which would imperil the whole of our civilization.

Twenty years later, Foerster, in his *Europe and the German Problem,* after precisely that world-wide growth of cynicism, wrote that the real mistake of 1918 was our concentration on politics and trade rather than on the dire necessity of marking an appalling crime for what it was, and bringing it home to the hearts and consciences of mankind.

Our scuttling of the truth in the interest of "appeasement" and our neglect to bring the crime home to the individual criminals had an inevitable effect on the minds of helpless millions in all countries. It produced

67

in them a kind of cynical despair, conscious or unconscious, of any possibility of the enthronement of conscience in politics and international affairs. They had
seen, as H. A. L. Fisher (statesman as well as historian)
wrote in his *History of Modern Europe*, the whole
world brought to the verge of war after war, in which
millions of lives, innocent of all knowledge of its causes,
would be lost, by the sole caprice of perhaps a single
tent'1-rate politician, with the morals of a gangster,
who had succeeded in setting his hand on the levers
of the political machine. (This was written before
Hitler had appeared on the scene.) They had seen us
eating our own words on the moral issue, after the war,
in our haste for "appeasement." They had seen us
pandering to our "pseudo-intellectuals" and adopting,
in the circles that form the mental fashions, a "Shavian"
attitude towards the blackest and bloodiest sins in history. If we were to be saved it could not have been by
intellectual snobbery. It could only have been by the
integrity of the ordinary people of Britain, the bourgeoisie so despised by the fashionable coteries of the
day; the quiet and forgotten average man, the man
in the street, who still read Dickens, and kept his
word, and, more often than not, believed in God; the
man, from whom — as the London *Times* suggested
recently — the pseudo-intellectuals will one day have
to learn the whole lesson of life anew.

Twenty years after a leading English journal had

The Edge of the Abyss

declared that no educated person any longer believes the record of the "Open Boats" outrages, of which we had moved heaven and earth to convince the world during the World War, British naval officers of absolute honesty were telling me that, with their own eyes, they had seen worse than the worst we had ever said of that German wickedness. The record to which the English journal referred was true in every detail. But we had invited our destruction by destroying our own credibility. The *Benares,* sailing westward, with a cargo of children, was sunk in mid-Atlantic; and the German wireless immediately exulted in the known fact that no deed now, however horrible, could evoke the natural reactions, even in the most generous hearts. It would merely make, as they said, "a good tear-jerking story" against which, by our own teaching, and by the sneers of the pseudo-intellectual cynics at every honest emotion that had ever stirred the human race, the whole world was now forearmed and hardened and "educated."

Nothing has more sickened the souls of those who can still think and feel than the growth of cruelty in recent years — a direct result of this "education" in cynicism. The communiqués of the gangsters, to whom we obligingly accord their own self-flattering descriptions (the "High Command," or the "Supreme Council" and, perhaps, presently, the "Almighty Gods"), no longer seek to minimize the bestial part of their work. They dwell upon it with exultation, as the most helpful part of their spiritual attack.

> *Our bombers left a trail of incredible destruction. They devastated the whole countryside and left village after village in ashes. The population was mercilessly machine-gunned and completely annihilated.*

That is invented, but it might appear in any totalitarian *communiqué*. It is the typical advertisement which they have discovered to be advantageous to themselves. Among the weak-minded it has even provoked admiration of the "great men," the "geniuses" (even though evil geniuses, nevertheless "great") who have loosed this wickedness on the world. There is certainly a temporary advantage in lying. There is certainly a temporary advantage with the man who has the gun in any civilized community. There is certainly no hypocrisy about it. Propaganda against the present leaders of Germany is certainly wasted now. Their own communiqués outblazon anything that we could say of them. They glory and exult in the shame of deeds at which the Inferno would shudder; and, in a world that has known Pasteur and Lister, Lincoln and Emerson, Dickens and Tolstoi, they become the "great men of the age" — wicked, perhaps, but "great," quite indubitably "great."

CHAPTER VII

It must not be supposed, however, that the spirit of this evil is an isolated phenomenon. It is active everywhere. It has been active in art and literature — through which the souls of nations are supposed to express themselves — for more than half a century, and in exactly the way described by John Buchan.

> There is in it all, too, an ugly pathological savour, as if a mature society were being assailed by diseased and vicious children.

It is just here that the enemy's most terrible victory may be found. For fifty years the pseudo-intellectuals have been preparing their way and making their paths straight by scoffing at every distinction between right and wrong in private human relationships, in marriage and in the home, as well as in wider spheres. In the name of art and the intellect, as you may see on almost every bookstall, they have reduced all human affections and emotions to the most primitive and brutal levels; and, since man cannot live unless he can at least pretend to have some ideals, they disguise "covetousness" and lust for power as humanitarianism and love of the proletariat, or desire for social reform.

71

The Edge of the Abyss

On the other side, we hear conservatives attacking Bolshevism as a menace to democracy; but we seldom hear it attacked on the true ground that, in its former doctrine, it obliterated the distinction between right and wrong, and deliberately reversed the eternal laws of God. It is far more than a political problem. It is an ethical problem affecting the whole conduct of human life. Moreover, the attack that has been made on all the standards of art and thought and conduct can be met by one power and one alone — the power of religion. It is only in the religion of Christendom that the distinction between right and wrong is derived from the very nature of the Supreme Being. It is only here that we find those reserves of true philosophic thought and, at the same time, the emotional fervor capable of delivering a complete answer to the disintegrating processes of materialistic thought in the modern world. Unless that answer is given there is no hope for humanity. Victory by force of arms will be as futile as it was in 1918, and the only result achieved by the war will be the millions of our dead.

For a great part of the world, the authority of conscience — that God within the breast — has been lost. "Conscience," said Hitler, "is a Jewish invention." He had evidently not heard of Socrates. But we must not expect too much of these "great political leaders," the tenth-rate quality of whose minds is one of the most startling facts in the present situation. But we were told, with bland persuasiveness, by our pseudo-intellectuals that, when we had given up our religion and ceased to draw distinctions between good and evil, we should be more tolerant one of the other. Some people even believed that toleration of the commonest kind of immorality — which usually means only moral indifference — would mean that the world would grow more kindly, more just, more merciful, more compassionate. They had forgotten those bitterly disillusioned lines of the poet Burns:

> I waive the quantum o' the sin,
> The hazard o' concealing;
> *But, oh! it hardens a' within,*
> *And petrifies the feeling!*

Those lines were as true as death and judgment to the real facts. In a nutshell they offer full testimony. They suggest the lying and deceit which are nearly always forgotten in the more romantic accounts of the kind of sin about which Burns was writing, and they also directly state the certain fact that the sensualist becomes all hardened within, loses all real capacity for human affection, breaks his pledges, reduces himself to a subhuman level; and, in fact — while actually living — tastes the wages of sin which is death to all the real values.

It is precisely this that has been happening to a large

part of the pseudo-modern and pseudo-intellectual world as it expresses itself (with "an ugly pathological savour") through literature and art. "Pseudo-modern," I say, because there is really nothing older than chaos; and "pseudo-intellectual" because its values are far below the level of the intellectual achievements of the race in literature and philosophy. In much of the work produced by them, "brutality" is mistaken for strength; and, indeed, the word "brutal" is one of their favorite adjectives of praise. The human affections, all those kindly human relationships which in the work of a great novelist like Dickens make up the real values of life, seem hardly to exist at all for the pseudo-intellectual. The more brutal passions which are common to the animals they seem to understand — as far as they go. But, for years, they have taken a peculiar and almost malicious pleasure in sneering the ordinary human affections out of existence. The kingdom of "the broken heart and the unbroken word," which is the Kingdom of God, means nothing to them.

This "world-wide attack" has not been without its effect. Nothing — it may be repeated — has more startled the believers in mechanical progress than the increase of cruelty and callousness in recent years. A few years ago, in the last war, a shudder of horror went through the world at the sinking of a single liner, without warning. Today, in the very face of international law, it is almost taken for granted that, if the totalitarian gets a chance, he will sink ships conveying hundreds of innocent little children, without warning, and with no more compunction than if he were drowning vermin. But, almost worse than the sinking of the *Benares*, as a symptom of what has been happening to our civilization, was that announcement which went out from Berlin shortly afterwards. The last of those little drowning hands had hardly ceased to wave this noble world good-bye, the last of these little voices had hardly been stifled in the black Atlantic, before Berlin flashed the message round the world: *"This will make a good tear-jerking story."*

They knew what they were doing. The effect of that wicked sentence was calculated by expert psychologists. It was a deliberate assault on the human soul. They knew how well the ground had been prepared by the brutal cynicisms of modern writing all over the world. They knew that they could appeal to the new toughness created by our intellectual fashions. They knew that their doings had intimidated the natural reactions of what used to be called "righteous anger," now so thoroughly "out of date" and ridiculous.

Our official counterblasts are useless. Our moral failure in the past, our attempts to "appease" by scuttling the truth, have not "appeased." They have destroyed a great part of our credibility; and they would have destroyed it entirely if it had not been for the inexorable logic of events. Thousands of the young, in American universities, for instance, as well as in our own, now suspect a lying propaganda in the very face of Truth itself, and are more cynical with regard to the English cause than most Englishmen at home suspect.

CHAPTER VIII

IT is because of the true and bitter feeling that we are all once again in danger of being deceived by false sentiment, or by high-sounding words which will be eaten as soon as the danger is past, with a supercilious *"no educated man any longer believes this,"* that the youth of America has so long doubted the light in the very eyes of truth.

An article in an American newspaper, expressing the feeling of American youth in the colleges, deserves to be read and studied by every older man in the English-speaking world. It is infinitely closer to the truth than that posthumous letter of a young airman which was circulated so widely in an endeavor to persuade a confused public that war was a blessing in disguise, since in peace all you could do was to eat and sleep and breed.

The unknown writer of this letter may have been one of the heroes and victims of our day, and the words may have been wrung from him by the general falsity of our time. It is even possible that by now "no educated man believes" in his existence.

It remains true that nothing more dreadfully symptomatic of what our time had done to the young was ever printed. Rupert Brooke was, at least, able to envisage a sacrifice for the young who died and left no children:

> . . . and those who would have been,
> Their sons, they gave, their immortality.

But we have advanced since then. That a young man should be almost glad of the horror that had descended upon mankind because, if it had not come, there would have been nothing for him to do but to eat and sleep and breed, is a formidable statement to circulate as "propaganda," in a world that had once known the glories of science and art and literature and religion; the happiness of love; the joy of little children; and the worship of God. So many worlds, so much to do!

People shed tears over it, and well they might. But they did not see the real tragedy of it, or visualize the utter falsity of their own feeling. Why worry about the world, if this war is better than anything else you could have. In any case, if it weren't for Hitler, you could do nothing but eat and sleep and breed.

American youth, apparently, did have something to look forward to, even in a world of peace. One of their own college presidents put it this way:

> Ten years ago the popular market was being flooded with books about the part propaganda played in war-time; and the British peer who headed that bureau for England, prior to our entry into the World War, wrote

The Edge of the Abyss

a book in which he took full and probably exaggerated credit for having brazenly manufactured pro-Ally sentiment in the United States to the point where we were actually fooled into going in on their side.

Unwisely, nothing was done to offset this talk. You and I remember the World War and how this college went. Those boys were neither "suckers" nor fools. They marched forth sincerely and honorably, and they lived or died gallantly. Their college is proud of them and reveres them. But, foolishly, we let all this belittling pass without speaking a word in defense of their ideals and sacrifices. We left them branded as "suckers" instead of what they were — loyal American patriots, courageous gentlemen and national heroes.

The peace-petitioning college student [continues the article] is no less courageous or loyal than his predecessors. . . . Confused, amazed . . . utterly and completely let down as the whole universe of his instruction swims suddenly in a hopeless whirlpool. All he's been taught and told to expect has suddenly gone into a blackout, leaving him unsupported and alone.

They gave him theory, ideals. Culture, and the sublime power of reason over brute force were drilled into him. The pattern of civilization, love of beautiful things . . . the mission, the opportunity to help straighten out with reason and intelligence the tangled affairs of a world that was failing from a lack of both. And now they're trying to hand him a gun and say: "Forget all that other stuff. It's just a lot of bunk now. Take this and go out and shoot a lot of people. You may get killed yourself, of course, or blinded, or crippled for life, but it's just one of those things." And this after years of telling him that this is

79

precisely the way not to settle any argument; that all war is futile.

If war never settled anything before, they say, why will it settle anything now?

If the other words were right before, why aren't they still right?

If education merely adds up to shooting somebody and getting shot, what was the use of going to college? The biggest moron ever born can pull a trigger. He probably can pull it better, for he has no imagination. Just destroying things, even life, can give him a thrill. Why books? Why music? Why the wisdom and beauty and fine things of the ages if the end of it all is to die in a savage conflict? It's all been a waste of time and money and dreams. They called the other the real way, the sort of life a man wants to lead, with a wife, some kids, and a home. If they were right before, why aren't they still right?

And when they see the presidents of their colleges and their prominent alumni, who have lectured them upon their great opportunities for service in a peaceful civilization, of the evils and futilities of dictatorial ideologies, suddenly, upon the public platform, urging the swift regimentation of all industry, a compulsory draft of all manpower, the terrific arming under what amounts to a super dictatorship, and another "idealistic crusade". . . . I'm not applying sarcasm to the exhorters, but endeavoring to show how it must look to these college lads.

No honest mind can fail to understand their despair of an "idealism" that our intellectuals annihilated. In the background, advertised and aided by the British press, there is Mr. Wells with his *The Fate of Homo*

The Edge of the Abyss

Sapiens telling them that the British Empire has "out-lived its usefulness," at the very moment when the salvation of human freedom depends upon it.

And, hanging over the whole thing, there are such things as that supercilious utterance in one of our greatest conservative newspapers, at the end of the last war, cynically dismissing the "Open Boats" outrages (which were as true as death and judgment): *"No educated man any longer believes this."*

The Irish in America have been confirmed in their beliefs about England by our literary fashions. It is certainly bewildering to an American reader to read quotations from our leading literary columns describing an Irish author as one of our greatest and then to find that the author aforesaid is accusing the British Government of criminal forgery of documents. One such book is on sale in New York at this moment. I am not attempting here to pass judgment on any particular case, but we cannot eat our cake and have it, in that fashion. It certainly does not have an "appeasing" effect, or convince those whose countrymen have been shot, to be told that we are gallant and generous "sportsmen" — the ostrich-like conviction of all English editors who allow truth to be treated as a "bourgeois virtue," and every loyalty to be ridiculed as "out of date." It has fed the hatred; and, indeed, I do not see how any patriotic Irishman could fail to hate us, if what our intelligentsia say of such books, in the literary columns of conservative papers, be true. It does not help either English or Irish literature for the Oxford University Press to invite an Irish Free State Senator to edit its collection of modern English poetry, fill it with the productions of the men who hated England, and add a special tribute to the charlatan now broadcasting against us from Italy. Mr. Churchill, in his *Great Contemporaries*, it may be remembered, tells us how the pseudo-intellectuals contributed to the downfall of at least one European power. Cheap flag-waving may be hateful and harmful, but supercilious contempt for all the loyalties is not the remedy. It has been extremely helpful to the crooked propagandists of "real politics" in Europe, when they tried to persuade American youth that, in the present struggle, it was mere hypocrisy to speak of right and wrong, or that (as a writer in the *Harvard Crimson* remarked recently) in this war both sides were equally at fault; or that, as Mr. Wells remarked, in his *The Fate of Homo Sapiens*, Mr. Chamberlain was more cunning and unscrupulous than any of the dictators. The remark was not quoted in the English conservative press; but the chief English literary columns puffed the book on the day of publication, and with this flourish of English trumpets it came to the United States, to be read, marked and inwardly digested. If it had been true, Mr. Wells ought to have been even more liberally garlanded; but, in that case, our political columns for months past had been deceiving their readers; and those journals, which, like the *Evening Standard*, had so wholeheartedly endorsed the policy of Mr. Chamberlain, had been doubly unscrupulous. It was not true. Mr. H. G. Wells was smearing an honest man who had simply been trying to save the world from war. But, again, we cannot eat our cake and have it. We cannot pay tribute to the false gods of the pseudo-intelligentsia and retain the respect of those who still cherish "that bourgeois virtue, truth."

CHAPTER IX

THERE is only one foundation upon which sanity can be restored to modern thought and security to modern civilization. It happens also to be the only foundation upon which the freedom of the individual and the "security of minorities" (Acton's test of a free country) can be established and reconciled with orderly government and the principles of true authority. It happens also to be the only foundation upon which the imperatives of ethics become absolute, though it should be towards a minority of only one. It is, therefore, the only answer to the proven fallacies of the totalitarian creed and the doctrine that there is no power above the State.

The greatest in mind and character of the historians who have used our tongue, and the profoundest of all who have written on human freedom, stated it thus:

> *There is a Will superior to the collective will of man, and a law that overrules those of Solon.*

It is only in the religious philosophy, the *philosophia perennis*, of Christendom that this great reconciliation is achieved — the reconciliation between the just authority of the State and the freedom of the individual soul in an eternal Reality which is the origin and end of both.

Bereft of this, the world of today cannot survive. Three or four sentences, and a quotation, towards the end of John Buchan's autobiography, will indicate here how one practical and well-balanced mind, whose natural optimism would certainly have made him reluctant, and indeed did make him reluctant, to accept any unhopeful conclusion, was nevertheless profoundly disturbed by the signs of the times. There had been a world-wide pseudo-intellectual attack he observed, in every department of art and letters, on the fundamental principles of ethics and religion, as well as on the most elementary codes of good faith and decency in ordinary human life; and this attack had preceded and prepared the way for the new savagery in the political world. There is a real and vital connection between these phenomena.

> The European tradition [he wrote] has been confronted with an Asiatic revolt, with its historic accompaniment of janissaries and assassins. There is in it all, too, an ugly pathological savour, as if a mature society were being assailed by diseased and vicious children.

Nobody who has followed recent developments in literature and the arts all over the world can fail to recognize the applicability of this description, or the truth of the diagnosis.

The Edge of the Abyss

He affirms, too, in the same connection, his belief that, bereft of its religious foundations, our civilization cannot endure. We still conventionally speak of it as a Christian civilization; but — as he also affirms — it is only in name a Christian civilization today. *"The Faith is being attacked, and the attack is succeeding."*

He quotes the words of one of the greatest of English statesmen, written seventy years ago:

I am convinced that the welfare of mankind does not now depend on the State and the world of politics; the real battle is being fought in the world of thought, where a deadly attack is being made with great tenacity of purpose and over a wide field upon the greatest treasure of mankind, the belief in God and the Gospel of Christ.

With this testimony, which John Buchan brought up to date and applied to our own time, we may return for a moment to the theme of the article, written twenty-four years ago, on those ugly pathological symptoms which had already begun to prepare the way and make the path straight for *Mein Kampf* and all that was implied therein.

In the pseudo-intellectual art and literature of the day, I suggested, we could see for ourselves all those destructive forces actually at work, sapping and mining, attacking all that had been built up by Christendom, and carrying a large part of the crowd with them on a wave of primitive brutality which, by both the crowd and the critics, was mistaken for "strength." These things were praised in literary columns, partly because of that crude mistake, but sometimes with the peculiar malice of those who were out to destroy the culture and literary tradition of a system or a nation that they hated. They were praised in a large part of the press because they were thought to have "publicity value," though they certainly did not represent the real mind of the public. The average man was often disgusted by them though, being unorganized and inarticulate, he could not express his disgust effectively, even when a leading newspaper committed itself to such extremes as *"the very obscenity of this book is somehow beautiful, and, if this is not great art, what is?"*

I think that some of us could deliver the answer. These symptoms of a profound disease did not escape observation; but the tendency in England has always been to regard intellectual conditions as of no practical importance. England, however, was warned again and again by at least the voice of Kipling which will be heard long after the language it used has gone the way of the language used by Martial, and left to the world only its immortal part. Kipling recognized the apparent insignificance of the "germ in the blood"; but what he said was as incisive and true in diagnosis as any epigram of the Roman poet.

The Edge of the Abyss

For instance, read "A Pict Song," first published as one of the incidental poems in *Puck of Pook's Hill*, that matchless series of story-cameos of the history of Britain.

Here the Picts, the Little Folk, conscious of their inferiority to the Romans, give voice to their malicious hatred of their rule, and gloat over the mischief little folk can do to the great ones and the collapse which will be sure to come. "We are the worm in the wood. We are the rot at the root!" they gleefully chant, comparing themselves to the mistletoe which smothers the oak it lives on, to rats gnawing a ship's cables and to moths ruining a noble garment, with the final exulting threat: "But *you* — you will die of the shame, And then we shall dance on your graves."

CHAPTER X

DURING a visit to Rome in 1938, I happened to meet the German Ambassador to Italy at a dinner. Later in the evening I had a conversation with him, which turned on the attitude of the German Government towards religion. I asked him about this; and, to my amazement, he uttered with considerable fierceness these memorable words: "The Catholic Church is in a much weaker position than it realizes."

He made it quite clear that weakness (by which he meant inability to hit back physically) was a good reason for attacking it. I ventured to question whether it was "weak" in other respects; and, at once, in his own degree, he adopted the Hitlerian technique. He looked as if he would burst with anger and then, with a purple face, rapped out: *"Germany will never tolerate a State within the State."*

Further, he made it quite clear that no form of Christianity, unless it were completely subordinated to the secular rulers of the State would be allowed to survive.

But, though the attack may be succeeding temporarily, I believe that the universal church is far stronger in intellectual resources than its opponents realize. There are vast reserves in its treasuries of thought and philosophy. The difficulty is to bring them into effective action against the confused and often nonsensical philosophies of our time. The majority of the merely literary critics are almost unaware of their existence. I wonder, for instance, how many of them have ever glanced at that magnificent translation of Godet by the late president Dwight, of Yale. There is a depth of thought, an exquisite subtlety, a profound learning, couched in the most sincere and beautiful style; and, in the face of work like this, the literary columns babble of the "erudition" of an Ezra Pound, whose blunders in his Latin and Greek tags are the laughingstock of every scholar. Godet is not out of date, and President Dwight's work upon him still makes the "higher critics" of Christianity look feeble. But the feeling of the German Ambassador about religion — as crude and elementary a feeling as any I have heard expressed — is typical of the contemporary materialism on all sides, though in English-speaking countries, with their greater regard for individual freedom, the pagans do not so much attack the Faith. They prefer to pick the mortar out of the walls and let them crumble.

And here, once again, I can only give examples of how the intelligentsia have played their part, in many cases quite unconsciously, but not without serving the purposes of shrewder men than themselves.

When Mr. Mencken writes to a friend that "Rabelais was nearer God than Christ," he was, of course, just

The Edge of the Abyss

being Mr. Mencken (which is to say partly Mr. Shaw). Mr. Shaw had said earlier that no man who regarded Christ as an ideal was worth working with — a statement so obviously foolish (since it eliminated millions of the finest minds and characters of the human race) that it needs no comment. But it must be noted that Mr. Shaw was ready to write a preface for a book by the late Mr. Frank Harris.

The habit of mind induced by the tone of such statements as those quoted above, and admired by the would-be "smart," undoubtedly prepared the way for the more serious attack. They are merely examples of a wide-spread habit.

One knows, of course, what Mr. Mencken meant. Rabelais was undoubtedly nearer to the modern critics' type of reality — the farmyard and the manure heap. There is no false sentiment about that; and, after all, God made the farmyard, and the filth, and the fat sow wallowing in it.

It is useless to answer this. If we did, we should be met with the reply that we are stupid not to see that "truth is merely a bourgeois virtue," and that Mr. Mencken was trying to shock the bourgeoisie. It is an attempt that doesn't seem to make much sense in this kind of connection.

One could hardly expect the pseudo-intellectuals to have any feeling for what a German philosopher once called "*das heilige*"; but one may call attention to the difference of outlook, tone and manners, between such utterances and those of free American thinkers like Fiske and Emerson. I have no wish to make a particular scapegoat of any contemporary exponent of the new smartness. But in a great many of them, this attitude of mind, this crude disrespect for anything higher than themselves, did actually prepare the way for the attack in its more direct forms. The sappers and miners had done their work. The mortar had been picked out of the walls; and the consequent world-wide moral and intellectual collapse made the way straight for the more forthright exultation of the *Hitler Youth Song:*

> We are the merry Hitler youth
> We need no Christian virtue . . .
> We follow not Christ but Horst Wessel;
> His Church can go take a running jump;
> The Swastika makes me happy on earth.

When civilized man has once had his roots cut, it is the moods of the hour that will rule him and sway him.

"When in centuries to come, mankind sees the present events in their true proportions, they will say: 'Christ was great, but Adolf Hitler was greater.' " That is what Becker, a leader of the German Labor Front, prophesied; and the spirit of his prophecy was exactly that of the pseudo-intellectuals, except that there was less malice in them and the German displayed more respect for the founder of the Christian religion.

94

The Edge of the Abyss

And now, lest my remarks on Mr. Mencken be supposed to lay too much stress on utterances which do not fairly represent the pseudo-intellectual atmosphere of our time, let us hear what a typical member of the younger intelligentsia has to say about the literary position of the man who thought Rabelais "nearer God than Christ."

This is what Mr. Edmund Wilson thinks of him: "He is the civilized consciousness of modern America, its learning, its intelligence and its taste, realizing the grossness of its manners and mind."

Mr. Edmund Wilson has, perhaps, more right than I to speak of his own country. But I should not have thought that the tone of the remark about Rabelais and Christ was characteristic of the civilized consciousness of America. I have met many of the religious leaders of America, and I certainly had the impression that they were not only "civilized," but men who could put most of the pseudo-intellectuals in one of their vest pockets. They had a far wider and deeper intellectual background than is to be found in any of the literature which can be regarded as characteristic of the contemporary intelligentsia. As for "manners," we can surely trust what was said by Mr. Mencken's very capable critic-friend, Mr. Untermeyer, to whom the remark "Rabelais was nearer God than Christ" was addressed.

Mr. Mencken may have been justified in heading

his letters during the World War with the words *"Gott strafe England."* He has expressed elsewhere his hatred of democracy. "But," says Mr. Untermeyer, "he usually ended piously with 'Yours in Christ.'" There are many millions of more intelligent men and women than Mr. Mencken who would regard that as exactly what it is — a crude imitation of one of the less pleasing tricks of Voltaire in his otherwise brilliant correspondence.

Here are some other specimens which I venture to think infinitely below the level of any real American thinker, Dr. Mortimer Adler, for instance, or Mr. Walter Lippmann, or a man of science like Dr. Millikan who, after all, won the Nobel Prize, so has some claim to be regarded as part of the civilized consciousness of America. Mr. Untermeyer says that Mr. Mencken, "while the Y. M. C. A. was uplifting the boys in France," himself referred to Christmas as the "birthday of your late co-religionist, Dr. J. C. Josephsohn."

Mencken never insisted on the honesty of invective as long as the diatribe was sufficiently thumping and calculated to stir up the animals.

It was characteristic of him that he issued a *Schimpflexikon* about himself: an extraordinary collection of catcalls, billingsgate, venom, lies, lampoons, larrupings, ugly names, uglier insinuations, and downright obscenity.

The Edge of the Abyss

Now, if this be true, and if the tone and manner of the references to the founder of the Christian religion do really emanate from one who is "the civilized consciousness of modern America, its learning, its intelligence and its taste" — as Mr. Edmund Wilson says — then America, rightly or wrongly, has ceased to be a Christian nation; not only ceased to be a Christian nation, but it must have lost a great many other things, including common honesty and common decency. It is utterly false, of course, but, if what Mr. Mencken himself says about "democracy" were true, the whole democratic façade would be as rotten with hypocrisy as are the constant public references by leading American statesmen to the Christianity of their country, and to the God whom they assert their country still worships. Several presidents of the United States, for instance, have openly stated that they believed in the ten commandments. This to the intelligentsia, and many of their followers on college campuses, would apparently be an incredible *naïveté*.

If the intelligentsia are right, then the abyss is unescapable. If they are wrong — as I believe they are — they are nevertheless, by all the methods described above, undermining the perilous edge on which the whole cultural tradition of Western civilization is fighting for its last foothold.

CHAPTER XI

To PUT it quite plainly, it is a question of character, not aesthetics, when we consider the kind of thing that has come to be accepted by many of the intelligentsia in recent years. Men of the calibre of Lincoln, Emerson, Fiske, Hawthorne, would not have written letters of facetious reverence, mocking at Christ, to a fellow writer who was about to speak in a college chapel. The literary columns, however, have sold the pass to the enemy; and, though they do not openly support the doctrines of the enemy, they have created a mental fashion in which to oppose them is to be "conventional," "out of date," and all the rest of the intimidating clichés, so beloved of the pseudo-intellectual.

The collapse is intellectual as well as moral. I think it is true, as Paul Elmer More once remarked to me, that the ability to think clearly and deeply has been vanishing from all sections of the modern world except those that have some grasp of the philosophy of religion, as it has been developed through two thousand years in the central tradition of Christendom.

There are obvious practical advantages in the use and development of what has already been achieved, and in not having to begin afresh at the beginning every few weeks. But the tree must be judged by its fruits; and the fruits of elementary fallacy among the contemporary intelligentsia are worthy of Lewis Carroll. Here is one example, which may relieve any suspicion that Mr. Edmund Wilson is likely to be right in what he says about "the American consciousness."

In *The Atlantic Monthly* for February, 1941, he wrote an article entitled "The Kipling That Nobody Read." In this article he attempted to psychoanalyze that great writer, attributing certain characteristics of his mature work to certain experiences of his childhood. It is difficult enough for an expert psychiatrist to arrive at any precise conclusions about a patient whom he is able to observe and question directly. But Mr. Wilson had no hesitation about his analysis of the most hidden motives of a mind so very much bigger and deeper than that of the usual patient — or doctor. He had never even met the patient; and his results — to anyone who had known Kipling — were, frankly, unrecognizable. In this, however, he has all the freedom of the subconscious in which to play about and fish for monstrosities, and he cannot be caught and pinned down. Fortunately, in the same article, he strays into the realms of the demonstrable; and there we have him on the hip. He discusses a story of Kipling's entitled "The Edge of the Evening." It was written in 1913, and the title was significant. It tells of two hostile airmen who had flown over England for reconnoitering purposes, and had made a forced landing in the grounds of an English country house. The English owner of

the house and an American guest came upon them un-
expectedly. The hostile airmen immediately shot at
them with intent to kill. The American promptly laid
out one of the airmen with a golf club (the only
weapon which he had ready), while the Englishman
collared the other with a football tackle and accident-
ally broke his neck.

Mr. Edmund Wilson describes all this in detail,
including the fact that the German airmen had been
armed and actually shooting; and then makes this
monumental comment: *This shows, he says, that in
Kipling's mind, lawlessness is justifiable when practised
by Englishmen and Americans.*

It is quite impossible to make any comment. But it
is there, in cold print, in *The Atlantic Monthly* for
February, 1941. It is a perfect example of how conservative journals in their anxiety to be "abreast of the
times" do aid the disintegrating process, and — instead
of exercising their proper critical functions — run
blindly after what they believe to be the "fashion."

In the same article it was asserted that Kipling's
reputation had declined during the last decade or two,
in comparison with that of admittedly minor writers.
But the question then arises: *Declined among whom?*
I happened to be present at Kipling's funeral in Westminster Abbey, where he was laid to rest by the side of
Dickens. None of the intelligentsia of the "literary"
world was there, though there were one or two good

writers. But the Abbey was packed from end to end with *men*: men who had done things; men who had built ships and governed countries; men with minds of their own. The Prime Minister of England was there, as one of the pallbearers; and the great silent crowd made, beyond all comparison, the most impressive tribute to any writer that had been made since the deaths of Tennyson and Browning. There was something prophetic about the deep-voiced words that echoed from the choir in that historic shrine:

> The tumult and the shouting dies;
>   The captains and the kings depart:
> Still stands Thine ancient sacrifice,
>   An humble and a contrite heart.
> Lord God of Hosts, be with us yet,
> *Lest we forget — lest we forget!*

I know that among the pseudo-intelligentsia, the very quotation of those words, the first glimpse of them on the printed page, irrespective of the context, would cause a titter, a snigger, or a sneer. But that is merely the final proof of the general inability of the pseudo-intellectual to get outside his own immense conceit of himself. "Fame" and "reputation," as they are estimated by such people would have seemed very little things to the author of those words. But even a member of the intelligentsia could hardly have imagined that he had gone down in the world, if he knew

that he would be laid to rest in Westminster Abbey,
in those circumstances. "That hateful smile of boundless self-conceit," as Browning called it, would perhaps
for half a second, vanish.

> Far-called, our navies melt away;
>   On dune and headland sinks the fire:
> Lo, all our pomp of yesterday
>   Is one with Nineveh and Tyre!

There are sets, of course, and sets; and it is the
incorrigible mistake of the intelligentsia, who think
and move only in sets, to believe that they are the
people and that wisdom is born and dies with them.
None of them was present in Westminster Abbey.
None of them therefore could see what was to be seen.
But, unhappily, they do occupy the literary columns,
and thereby confuse values to a degree that was impossible when the great central tradition of Western
culture provided rational standards of judgment.
Exactly the same mistake of contemptuous dismissal
has been attempted by the intelligentsia in the case
of greater writers, from Virgil to Tennyson, in recent
years; and the spirit of the attack is precisely that of
an urchin throwing a stone through a cathedral win-
dow, and defending himself by saying that the cathedral is not abreast of the times. Mr. Walter Lippmann,
one of the soundest and clearest-thinking of all con-

temporary American writers, in a recent address to which I shall return presently, remarked that "deprived of their cultural tradition, the newly educated western men no longer possess in the form and substance of their own minds and spirits, the ideas, the premises, the rationale, the logic, the method, the values, or the deposited wisdom which are the genius of the development of western civilization. The prevailing education is destined, if it continues, to destroy western civilization, and is in fact destroying it.

"Modern education rejects and excludes from the curriculum of necessary studies the whole religious tradition of the west. It abandons and neglects as no longer necessary the study of the whole classical heritage of the great works of great men.

"Thus there is an enormous vacuum where until a few decades ago there was the substance of education."

CHAPTER XII

FROM a merely literary point of view, there is hardly a fallacy in Lewis Carroll so ludicrous as some of the critical announcements printed today, especially among the explorers of the "subconscious mind." The critic who is quite ready to psychoanalyze the mind of Rudyard Kipling, without the slightest fear of getting out of his depth, blandly accepts the testimony of the late Mr. Arnold Bennett's diary on Kipling, and swallows whole the gossiping remarks of an otherwise unknown Mrs. Smith, as though these witnesses, together with the analyst himself, lived in a world entirely superior to any such examination, while the really big men are all to be put under the microscope. It never occurs to him that the late Mr. Bennett might also be psychoanalyzed, with amusing results, among which we should find considerable jealousy of the infinitely superior texture of Kipling's style. It never occurs to them that Mrs. Smith might also be psychoanalyzed. Her evidence was based on the remarkable fact that she was once a fellow passenger on a liner with Rudyard Kipling. Psychoanalysis *might* — I don't say it *would* (for I am not an expert like Mr. Wilson) — it *might* disclose that Kipling didn't want very much to have her settled next to him in a deck chair, talking hard, all the way from Portsmouth to Mandalay. God knows, and Mr. Wilson, who didn't know Kipling, knows; while I, who did know Kipling a little, frankly confess that I have no means of knowing, subconscious or otherwise. But we are overrun with exactly the same nonsense in England. A writer on Dickens recently tried the same foolish trick. In dealing with Mr. Pickwick's famous adventure, where he found himself in the old lady's bedroom at the White Horse Inn, he solemnly said that this revealed the secret sexual life of Dickens. It will be remembered that Mr. Pickwick, in his panic, had fled from the old lady's room, into which he had quite inadvertently strayed, and, in his hurried search for his own room, had tried several other doors by mistake. This passage, affirmed the subtle critic, could only have been written by a man who, in his past, had furtively turned the handles of many bedroom doors for an immoral purpose.

Could lunacy go further? The answer, alas, is "Yes, it can; and considerably further."

CHAPTER XIII

How near to Bedlam the pseudo-intellectuals have come may be briefly illustrated by a remark of Mr. H. G. Wells, concerning one of those esoteric "highbrow" periodicals which are so invariably wrong in all their ideas and utterances on art and literature, and so swiftly demoded. We will call it X.

The world at large wants a clear lead; and it is from the artists, writers and *teachers* to whom X appeals that plain directions must come, *if they are to come at all.*

So says Mr. Wells. The italics are mine. On the recommendation of so "major" a thinker, who limits the hope of the world to so few and so happy a band of brothers, one might well examine this valuable periodical. A stack of it recently fell into my hands and I examined it for light and leading.

A typical contribution was a long article on an alleged "modern poet" who was treated as of vast importance. Fourteen pages were devoted to him though, quite demonstrably, nobody could understand a single line of him, owing to the misuse of words and the complete disorder of the syntax. For instance, these from a sonnet on the Crucifixion, described in X as "his best."

The Edge of the Abyss

> This was the sky, Jack Christ, each minstrel angle
> Drove in the heaven-driven of the nails
> Till the three-coloured rainbow from my nipples
> From pole to pole leapt round the snail-waked world.

"Jack Christ" says the critic, in explanation, "is Hopkinsese. Christ is Everyman; *minstrel angle — ministering angel*, also literally *minstrel angle*, that is each corner of the singing sky." But then the verb "drove" must serve for both the angles and the angel, and, in either case, it makes absolutely no sense at all. The critic tells us that it also

> ... *symbolizes the birth of love through the death of sex.* ... *The conclusion to be drawn from this fine crucifixion poem is disturbing. After presenting in all his poems a brilliant sexual interpretation of life, he has here presented a sexual interpretation of death. The secret of death, and its horror, is that it is sexless.*

If these queer creatures be examples of the sex-endowed, any normal reader might well exclaim, "O death, where is thy sting!" Fortunately, they are not. The bait for the immature mind is merely that, floating about in this chaotic mess, there are constant vague suggestions of a sexual "imagery" or, as it would be truer to call it, a sexual leer, with an occasional dirty suggestion thrown in. It reminds one of the absurd incident recorded by Chesterton when Louis de

The Edge of the Abyss

Rougemont (the modern Baron Munchausen) went for a walk with him and, solemnly pointing to the spire of a village church, told the amazed Chesterton that it was really a subconscious sexual symbol. Chesterton went into a sudden convulsion of laughter, and continued to laugh about it, years later, till the tears rolled down his face.

But the crazy solemnity of these charlatans, and their solemn critical expositors, goes beyond anything in the former history of the world. Here are two more lines:

> The horizontal cross-bones of Abaddon
> Rung bone and blade, the verticals of Adam.

On which the critic in *X* quite seriously remarks: "*Why horizontals and verticals (genitals would do)?*"

He is not making a crude barrack-room joke. He is a high-brow, talking critically, to a race which had heard what Johnson, Wordsworth, Landor, Arnold and Saintsbury have had to say on the high function and destiny of the Art of Poetry. "*Genitals would do!*"

"However, the difficulties are not shirked," the enthusiastic critic continues. "All the horrors of birth [as suggested by Genesis and Milton perhaps] are conveyed in a brutally effective language":

The Edge of the Abyss

And love plucked out the stinging siren's eye,
Old cock from nowheres lopped the minstrel's tongue.
Till tallow I blew from the wax's tower
The fats of midnight when the salt was singing;
Adam, time's joker, on a witch of cardboard
Spelt out the seven seas, an evil index,
The bagpipe-breasted ladies in their dead-weed
Blew out the blood gauze through the wound of man wax.

Now I do not for a moment suggest that an expert in crossword puzzles might not discover some oblique allusion to some obscure branch of obstetrics in all this; or that those profound persons who "feel there is something in it" are not just as right as they would be if they said the same thing about an addled egg. What I am quite certain about is this: that it has no artistic value whatsoever; and that it is demonstrably impossible to extract any real meaning or thought from it. Demonstrably, I say, because the syntax, the language — structure whereby thought is conveyed — is nonexistent, and the punctuation of the passage merely emphasizes the lack of any organization of the ideas, if the ideas ever existed. If it is a picture of anything at all it is a picture of a mind in complete dissolution, as in softening of the brain.

But this is what the high-brow critic of X draws out of it, with the perfect ease of the complete humbug:

The Edge of the Abyss

The attending presence [he says] *of the siren and cock (both symbolize lust and sacrifice), Adam (the sinner), and the ladies in the dead-weed, against sirens, Fates, Furies, acting as mid-wives, heightens symbolically the horror of Christ's difficult, and indeed unnatural birth.*

Then, a page or two later, comes what is perhaps the most remarkable statement ever given to the reading public, outside the walls of a lunatic asylum. It was all printed on beautiful paper and exported to America, while grand old firms of publishers like Blackwood and Murray were unable to obtain adequate supplies for serious literature. I regret having to offer the specimen that follows; but, if the specimens were not shown, the extent of the mental collapse would seem incredible, outside the ranks of the intelligentsia.

The imagery of this poet [says the admiring critic] *is predominantly masculine, to the point of onanism and homosexuality.*

Strange evidence of masculinity. I need hardly say that the evidence is not openly given in the eminent journals where this stuff is solemnly regarded as literature. The serious aspect of the matter is that eminent journals should play the fool in this way with the greatest literary inheritance that has been vouchsafed to any people in any language.

The Edge of the Abyss

Side-by-side with these [the enthusiastic critic contin-
ues] *are other equally male sex-images, which convey
also the idea of death and disgrace, such as the slug, the
snail and the maggot."*

Writing of this kind is perfectly familiar to alienists.
But there has been nothing hitherto like the ludicrous
academic earnestness of these sentences in any literary
criticism known to history.

Unhappily, in a world which is increasingly accus-
tomed to parrot its opinions and even its language from
the latest catchwords of press or radio (so that twenty
million persons will be talking of their "frustrations" in
April, who had never heard of the word in March),
it imposes on a certain number. "After all," as an
earnest educator said to me once, "there is so much
more of the subconscious mind, isn't there? It must
be more important than the conscious." The answer
to that is, fortunately, simple. The steersman and the
steering gear of a great ship may be only a small part of
it; but, if it is abandoned to the dreams or nightmares
of the sleeping passengers below, the ship will not
reach its destination.

The offensive matter in all this folly has little to do
with morality or its opposite. There has been no lack
of dirt in any generation. But this almost imbecile
high-brow solemnity — there is no other word for it —
does indicate a degeneration. Indeed, on one occasion,

when I had been engaged in a public debate with one of the exponents of this "new literature," a keen-faced man who had been sitting in the front row approached me at the close and gave me his card.

"I thought you might like to know," he said, "that I came here today for scientific reasons. I wanted to have a good look at your opponent. Many of my patients have been turning out stuff which I find quite indistinguishable from his."

The card was that of one of the most eminent of modern alienists, and he showed me specimens which were, in fact, indistinguishable. It has given me considerable pleasure to observe the look of uneasiness on the faces of those who profess to admire such stuff, when they have been challenged, subsequently, to distinguish between the work of the patients, and the truly modern "poets."

Another typical contribution to the high-brow periodical is a story, in prose this time, of how a young girl, Judith, enjoys the great privilege of "Meeting the Master" (i. e., the late Mr. D. H. Lawrence whose nervous system has been so enthusiastically explored by so many morbidly inane young women).

Two elderly spinsters had been invited to tea. This is how the host and the young girl behave; and particular attention may be called to the words *kindly*, *cruelty*, *coarse*, *possessively* and *malicious*, in the passage which I am about to quote, because those words illustrate the

The Edge of the Abyss

semi-insane perversity of what follows. Again, I regret to have to offer the specimen; but there is a growing habit in literary columns of praising and exalting these things, exactly as Mr. Wells praises and exalts the "writers and teachers" to whom they appeal, without quoting the operative passages which are the real bait for unwary and immature minds:

The Misses Smith, like as two peas, came into the room. In spite of the hot Italian sun, both were dressed in trim grey flannel suits buttoned tightly over their thin chests, both wore grey felt hats and carried, rather incongruously, bright parasols. Their kindly, faded faces lit with pleasure at the sight of Lawrence and he, a charming host, chatted and teased as he handed them tea and pastries and warmed them with his attentiveness. Judith was puzzled. For all his alleged hatred of humanity, Lawrence seemed to like them so much, these rather dull, prim and elderly Virgins. And they, though they spoke to him severely, as if he were some reprehensible small boy, were clearly delighted by him, blossomed and grew animated in his presence.

With instinctive cruelty the girl stretched in her chair, flaunting her fresh roundness, her uncreased youth. But the Virgins didn't notice; they were concentrated on Lawrence.

"Now look at the pictures," he said.

Obediently they rose and stood in front of the holy family. A young Joseph, dark faced, grinning slightly, dominated the picture, standing tall and rather coarse, with his arm possessively round Mary. And she leaned placidly against him, looking up, utterly careless of the child that was perched upon her knee. Like Judith, the Misses Smith were silent and it was clear that they, like her, didn't care for the picture. But Judith now veered passionately in defence of Lawrence's work. "Silly old things," she thought, and she said:

"Lovely, isn't it?"

The Virgins didn't answer.

When they came to the bevy of nuns, however, it seemed to please them better.

"But why did you put *him* in?" asked the elder Miss Smith, pointing to the figure of a peasant who peered derisively at the group from behind a corner of the convent. "He spoils it."

"Why, he's the whole point of the picture," said Lawrence laughing.

He went to a cupboard, brought out a sheaf of water colours and started to show them .

"That's good," said one Miss Smith, and the other agreed. Here was something they understood and, looking through the pile, they spoke as fellow artists, discussing, criticizing.

"Here's one I particularly like," said Lawrence. He grinned maliciously. "It's called 'Le Pisseur.' "

They all looked. "But why?" thought Judith. "Why? I don't see it."

The younger Miss Smith was the first to speak. She flushed.

"Really, Lawrence," she said. "You go too far."

Lawrence was furious.

"What do you mean?" he said. "I go too far? What's

wrong with the picture? Look at it. Look at that lovely curve. It's a lovely, natural thing."

But it was too much for the Virgins. They were really shocked and hurt.

"No, no, Lawrence," said the elder. "You shouldn't do these things. You really shouldn't."

After they had gone, Lawrence was still angry.

"The impudence," he said, "the incredible impudence. To speak like that to me. I'm a real artist and they take it on themselves to say things like that to me!"

"Oh, well," said Judith, secure in being all right, in understanding things a little, in her wholehearted allegiance to him. "Oh, well — the Virgins."

Lawrence paused. He looked at her, mocking, amused.

"You're the real virgin, you know," he said.

The infantile attempt to be "shocking" is hardly more impressive than the equally infantile "I'm a real artist." The smallest untrained dog could create a similar incident in any human habitation; but it seems an odd ambition, even for a pseudo-intellectual. The method here differs from that of the dog, however, in a way that connects it directly with the crazily sadistic manifestations in European concentration camps. First, it was done to insult simple and kindly people, with deliberate "malice," as the admiring chronicler tells us. ("Malice" and "brutality" are both laudatory words in these circles.) Secondly, the "malice" having provoked the natural remonstrance which it was intended to provoke, the gentleman then bursts into a Hitlerian rage really directed against the whole social structure and all its codes of courtesy and good manners. There are people who desire to do this, and our incompetent literary criticism has been aiding the process all along the line. I am giving merely instances, which may seem slight in themselves, but they could be multiplied by the thousand, and they are definitely characteristic of the "artistic" trend of our day.

It will be noted, too, that the picture of Joseph was intended to "smear" a sacred tradition. The real artist could have depicted a "coarse possessiveness" almost anywhere else, without any formidable indictment. But the vulgar leer of that phrase about the Mother of Christ is directly connected with the "world-wide attack upon the Faith" as Buchan called it, an attack which has been "succeeding" because too many people (including teachers and editors) have been intimidated into thinking they must agree with the "cliques" in order to be "abreast of the times," and that they must profess to admire what, at heart, all true men and women everywhere despise. It is impossible to exaggerate the gulf that exists between these "imposed" opinions of the literary columns, and the real tastes of true men and women everywhere.

I have personally tested this from a thousand platforms, and I have never failed to find the audience wholeheartedly with me, where the cliques of the literary columns would have said the exact opposite. "No one would dare to quote Longfellow in public today," said a fatuous English editorial recently. A year or two later, in the greatest crisis of human history, the President of the United States sent a message of encouragement to a nation fighting for its life, and the centre and heart of the message was a quotation from that despised poet —

> Humanity with all its fears,
> With all the hopes of future years,
> Is hanging breathless on thy fate!

Our editors, at the very moment when they think they are ahead of the times, are flopping behind them.

CHAPTER XIV

A GREAT literature has come perilously near to sliding into the Abyss. The effect of the attempts to corrupt it on the young and their talk, has been noted again and again by educationalists. For in recent years literature, that great instrument of education, that great means of spiritual communication, has actually fallen — to a larger extent than is generally realized — into the hands of men of tenth-rate character, who have been able to intimidate the better part of the community into accepting base standards, lest they should be ridiculed as being "out of date." That is the truth of the matter. To give an instance, in that very fine book, *The Flowering of New England*, a book full of atmosphere, and beautifully written, there was little need for the author to placate a contemporary fashion by accepting its cheap patronage of Longfellow, and deprecating the plain truth spoken by Lowell when he speaks of the bogus "realists" or the "discreditable curiosity" and "key-hole peeping" to which certain kinds of modern biography and fiction increasingly pander. Nothing could be more moderate or truer than Lowell's statement that "the so-called realist raises doubts in my mind when he assures me that he, and he alone, gives me the facts of life. . . . But are they the facts? I had much rather believe them to be accidental and transitory phenomena of our existence here."

Certainly the great Greek dramatists were able to enhance the effect of their great art by letting the bloodshed and the horror take place behind the scenes. Their skill in doing this has been praised for centuries by the greatest critics, not because it concealed facts, but because it concentrated the whole attention of the mind and spirit on the tragic significance of what was taking place, rather than on details of merely physical horror.

If we are now to keep the spiritual significance out of sight and continually call attention to the details of the lavatory (a habit increasingly common among hundreds of writers who seem to think that this, too, serves as "bait"), the whole lesson, not only of great criticism, but of elementary education, and the nursery, not to mention the common house-training of dogs, will have to be revised.

The civilized and sensitive have too long allowed themselves to be intimidated by these dull and dirty people. Plain speaking is necessary here. They impudently claim it for themselves, and we are entitled to give them the full measure of our own more civilized "reactions" in return. An Englishwoman, writing a novel about China, which obtained an American prize, painted a picture of English official life there, which, if true, would justify the Asiatic in a complete contempt for us and all our ways. It was not true. But there is one passage in it, in which one of the characters, an Englishwoman, tells an American woman that the manure used by the Chinese for their crops is the sewage of their cities. The manner of the telling is slightly disgusting, as it might be if told by a mannerless urchin. The American woman's face, for a fleeting moment, shows that this was her reaction. Whereupon, and this is the only point of my comment, the Englishwoman looks at her with "malicious" enjoyment of her embarrassment. The word "malice" is used exactly as it is used in the passage quoted above about D. H. Lawrence; and it is suggested that the Englishwoman is, in some subtle drawling way, superior to the American woman's dislike of "reality." Now, is it true that coarse talk about excrement is more "real" than the things that the human spirit seems more exquisitely adapted to appreciate? Is it really wrong to observe certain reticences? If so, why do we not change the architecture of our houses and bring the latrine into the dining room? And why "malice"? Why the very word for the spirit in which certain things have been done in the Nazi concentration camps? I have no more use for such "malice" in literature than I have for priggishness or prudery. But our best writers have shown far too much timidity towards these people and their clichés about "convention." It may be a convention not to spit in the soup at a dinner party. At the same time, we must insist on its observance, whatever the "reactions" may be. Deference and courtesy are treated as symptoms or confessions of weakness by these mannerless folk, and are therefore wasted on them. I spoke above of one of the most delightful pictures of New England and its life ever painted. The rich coloring and fine artistry of the writer, Mr. Van Wyck Brooks, are worthy of a conversation piece by Zoffany. But, towards the end of his book, he does make just this mistake of seeming a little too anxious to "appease" the opposite spirit in the life of our time. His deference and courtesy towards this spirit lead him to concede too much when he uses the words "conventional" and "narrow-minded" to describe one of the most just and exactly true utterances of that great critic — Lowell. It is not a sound argument to say in deference to Mr. Arnold Bennett and his clan, that Lowell was disingenuous in doubting whether the "facts" of the realists were the only reality, or thinking they might be transitory phenomena.

It will be noted that Lowell does not even dispute the reality of the "facts" of the realists. He merely doubts whether they are the *only* reality.

Could anything be more moderately and fairly stated? Yet, in deference to the crazy vanity of crude and ephemeral writers over whom, intellectually, Lowell towers out of sight, his remark has to be described as "narrow-minded," "conventional," and even "disingenuous," which in this case is a politer way of saying, "dishonest."

There is something almost comic, moreover, in the typical appeal to our fears for the future, and what the "revolutionary" young are going to do about it if we continue to say things like that. Mr. Brooks is, I think, far too ready to accept the argument that so moderate a statement by Lowell "was to breed a reaction in later generations, when the *cache-sexe* that emphasized the sex was rudely torn away, and the spotlight fell on the sex that had fallen on the fig-leaf."

There is certainly no sex emphasis of either kind in Lowell. Moreover, if a half-wit, posing as a genius, struts into our houses, and threatens to behave disgustingly unless we alter the tone of a perfectly rational conversation, we have a right, I think, to turn him out. Nor should we be intimidated by any threat that, if we do, the next generation will "react" by rolling like swine in the gutter.

In all this rather ludicrous and timid talk of possible "reactions" among people who, it seems to be assumed, have no self-control whatsoever, there is occasionally a recollection of some quite irrelevant injustice to a Keats or a Shelley. But this gambit has been played now for half a century, and only the very immature will now accept it. If the Pekinese misbehaves himself in my study, it is no use pleading with me to remember how we misunderstood Wagner.

The Edge of the Abyss

If our judgment and criticism are just, we need not be intimidated by the half-wits of the current fashion into apologizing for it, or placing Tennyson and Browning below the level of the late Mr. Oscar Wilde; or setting Fra Angelico below the level of the late Mr. Aubrey Beardsley. Here, however, is the sequence:

> The vilest of all pictures painted well
> Is nobler than the noblest painted ill;
> Nay, nobler than the noblest painted well
> So prone are we towards the broad way to hell.

There is certainly no *cache-sexe* in the work of Lowell any more than in Tennyson's *Oenone* and his picture of the choice of Paris:

> Naked they came to that smooth- swarded bower,
> And at their feet the crocus brake like fire,
> Violet, amaracus, and asphodel.

The difference is just that there is no infantile sniggering about it. The difference is between the beauty and splendor which constitute the purity of great Art, and the viciousness of the corrupt mind. The corrupt mind (we are constantly told by artists) cannot enter into the true artist's sense of form when he is depicting the beauty of the human body. This is either true, of the model and the studio, as well as of the art gallery, or else it is just Pecksniffian. I believe it to be true of all true artists. If it is not true, however, if the artist in his studio is, after all, a vicious little guttersnipe, leering "maliciously" at his visitors, we must still, it appears, "move with the time." But a great deal more than a "Victorian convention" will have slipped into the Abyss. A tradition of great Art, two thousand years old, will have gone, too — the very tradition which once set the great artist above the narrow decorum of the vulgar, on the very ground which is now rejected, that he was not concerned with mere animalism.

This does not preclude the representation in literature of physical passion. *Antony and Cleopatra; The Eve of St. Agnes; The Ordeal of Richard Feverel;* Tennyson's *Fatima* — all of them represent physical passion with the utmost frankness and with an intensity quite beyond the range of any contemporary writer. There is not a "heroine" in the most "realistic" of contemporary novels who — so far as physical passion goes — would not look like an anaemic little schoolgirl in her first "make-up" by the side of the Fatima of Tennyson. This isn't what the current critics say? Of course, it isn't. Half of them don't read and half of them can't read anything but what they might have written themselves; or, if they do read it, they read it with a preconceived idea that blinds them to the furnace of beauty under their very eyes. But these great representations of physical passion do not reverse or destroy the values by which the soul lives, either directly or by implication. Indeed by implication, and often by tragic implication, they reaffirm them. It is not the body, but the spirit that, with its passionate sense of the impermanence of all things here, utters the most beautiful line in Shakespeare:

Of many thousand kisses the poor last.

This, then, is not an argument against the representation of physical passion in its completeness. But it *is* an argument against the destruction of the real values of the individual soul, or making them contemptible; for this makes the way straight again for the enemy. He has no greater ally in this than the art and literature of the pseudo-intellectuals.

If human nature is really as it is depicted by some of our "realists," the State can do nothing better than use it as cannon fodder, in the interests of "real politics" without the slightest concern for any values of the individual soul.

"The subtlety of analysis could go no further," says an eminent novelist of Proust, whose ludicrous processions of sexual perverts surpass anything seen in Europe since the days of Nero, and would themselves (in view of the high position given to Proust) explain the downfall of France. One of his characters affirms that considerably more than half the members of French society were perverts of this type; and Proust, if his books are as true a picture as they are said to be by his "subtle" admirers, unconsciously signed the verdict and the death warrant. There is no escape from this position. If his books are false, then the intellectual hypocrisy of our time which has praised them as the most exquisite product of the modern civilized mind, is quite unfathomable. To revel in falsities of that sort stamps and brands its initiates; and, incidentally, what becomes of the "masterly" analysis? Analysis of a lie? If, on the other hand, he gives a true picture, then the Abyss is unescapable; unescapable for France, and for every relic of the rotten civilization which he repre-sents.

I believe his books to be as false as hell: false in char-acter; false in fact; false in atmosphere. But the bland hypocrisy of the literary praise which has been given to them is almost more nauseating than the work itself. The very word "Proust" has become a sort of synonym for the most exquisite literary caviare. Seldom or never do we see it openly stated in the literary columns, which pay their homage to him, all over the world, that the chief subject of his "subtlety" is the unnatural offences of fat and wealthy Frenchmen with bell-hops or penniless "artistic" aspirants; or offences against nature by women, of the kind described in the first chapter of the *Epistle to the Romans*.

I am not a moralist. I approached this matter merely as a man of letters. But the *Epistle to the Romans*, as the downfall of the ancient world began, so exactly describes the conditions of the world of Proust, and the consequences of those conditions, that the relevant passages may be quoted here. It may be noted that St. Paul is more frank than Proust. It is not a question of avoiding the subject. It is St. Paul who has the boiling temperament, and Proust who is the simpering prig. The difference between the author of the *Epistle to the Romans* and Proust is that the former is completely frank, and speaks from the depths of his spirit, showing what happens to men and women when they allow their higher faculties to be dethroned by an insurrection of the lower. Proust, on the other hand, not only takes a sniggering and debased pleasure in the degradation, but tries to convey that debased pleasure to others. The writer to the Romans deals with that very point:

Wherefore God also gave them up to uncleanness through the lusts of their own hearts, to dishonour their own bodies between themselves:

Who changed the truth of God into a lie, and worshipped and served the creature more than the Creator. . . .

For this cause God gave them up unto vile affections: for even their women did change the natural use into that which is against nature:

And likewise also the men, leaving the natural use of the woman, burned in their lust one toward another; men with men working that which is unseemly, and receiving in themselves that recompence of their error which was meet.

The Edge of the Abyss

. . . full of envy, murder, debate, deceit, malignity; whisperers.

Backbiters, haters of God, despiteful, proud, boasters, inventors of evil things, disobedient to parents.

Without understanding, covenantbreakers, without natural affection, implacable, unmerciful:

Who knowing the judgment of God, that they which commit such things are worthy of death, not only do the same, but have pleasure in them that do them.

And that — up till the outbreak of war in 1939 — was an exact description of a large pseudo-modern, pseudo-intellectual section of "European civilization" as revealed, and still on record, in Art and Literature.

It was by no means the whole of it, but it had usurped a disproportionate power in the critical columns; so that a large part of the press of the Western world praised these manifestations in a way that intimidated even educators, and led them to depreciate the real values of the great writers of the past, and those who endeavored to carry on and develop the great tradition into their own time.

An American critic, Professor Beatty, has demonstrated that this attack was fundamentally against every writer who had any ethical philosophy of life; and that it was essentially an attack of what Kipling called "the Bandar-Log," (monkey-folk) the representatives of an embittered mediocrity against better and bigger men than themselves. Their attack succeeded, temporarily,

129

by sheer dint of numbers, and even against outstanding men like Kipling. They bore him down, as a thousand monkeys might bear down Bagheera, the panther. But I remember how, on one occasion, a whole crowd of them, headed by the late Mr. Arnold Bennett, appeared in an English law court to protest that no literary evidence had been called when a certain novel, dealing with unnatural offences, had been condemned. Counsel for the public prosecutor thereupon turned his head, and Mr. Rudyard Kipling suddenly appeared.

"Do you still wish to call literary evidence in support of this book?" the magistrate quietly asked the counsel for the defence.

The crowd of pseudo-moderns took one look at Rudyard Kipling, and the counsel for the defence shook his head.

"Thank you, Mr. Kipling," said the magistrate. "I don't think you will be needed any longer."

And Kipling tiptoed quietly out of the court. It is quite possible that he would merely have quoted the *Epistle to the Romans*. But they were not prepared to face Bagheera.

CHAPTER XV

WE may be quite sure that if Lowell or Emerson were writing about an author like Proust they would at least have disclosed his subject matter. There would be no "*cache-sexe*" about it. But the critical journals of our time, though they constantly discuss him in tones of reverence, have been as reticent about the subject of his exquisite analysis as a society of Rosicrucians. Only occasionally does a less tactful critic find it difficult to repress a snicker.

It is at least refreshing to find Mr. Louis Untermeyer indirectly letting the cat out of the bag, without intending to do anything of the kind. It is usual for the "advanced" critics to deny with the utmost indignation the kind of charge which I have made against the work of men like Proust. The denial is usually couched in tones that suggest a low Philistinism in the maker of the charge, who is represented as vulgarly unaware of the superior beauties of the work in question. Now, whatever else one may say of him, nobody would suggest that Mr. Louis Untermeyer is "behind the times," in such matters, or that he would take a merely conventional point of view about such crucial figures of the pseudo-modern as James Joyce and Proust. And, indeed, he doesn't. When he was writing of the American poet, Sara Teasdale, in one little unguarded moment, he revealed to us the exact category in which he places the exquisite literary caviare of Proust and Joyce.

> *The modest Sara [he writes] learnedly discussed the sexual perversions in Proust. She read Joyce's* Ulysses *over and over and delighted in the concluding monologue of Mrs. Bloom. Although she scarcely specialized in pornography, she was the (unpublished) author of the most scatological quatrain and the lewdest Limerick I know.*

Mr. Untermeyer is not condemning these things — far from it. And this makes the testimony of his sub-conscious mind all the more valuable. The instances he gives must all hang together, or the sentences would have no connection. But Mr. Untermeyer certainly knows that, in modern critical circles, they would not be allowed to hang separately.

The lofty praise of *Ulysses* — that "foul chaos" as Edmund Gosse called it — will remain as an indelible stain on a system of criticism which has grown too corrupt, and too Pecksniffian, to realize its degradation or its hypocrisy. Mr. Untermeyer's remarks are, at least, in refreshing contrast with the pompous humbug of the pseudo-intellectuals.

A few journals, in the English-speaking world, still imply rather furtively, by allusion or supercilious assumption, that the book described by Gosse as a "foul chaos" is a masterpiece, more important than almost anything else in the literature of the last half century. This is partly because the editors do not know what it contains; but not always. I have in my possession a letter from the editor of one of the most famous newspapers in our language. It is in this paper that, in a long and prominent article, the book in question is described as a masterpiece of European literature. "Its very obscenity is somehow beautiful, and, if this is not high art, what is?" In the letter, which was written a few weeks later, and handed over to me by the recipient, the editor says, "*I have now read* Ulysses. *It is unspeakable.*"

But there was no public retraction, no atonement, no change in the public critical policy of the paper. The effect of this, and many other instances of the same kind, was to intimidate or bluff the more weak-minded in the educational world, with the result that this work, obscene beyond anything that has ever been printed, was even introduced into mixed college classes in "freshman English." One college professor informed me that he thought it was a good thing to "inoculate the young with evil" as a protection; and this was after one of the most experienced dramatic critics in the world had told me that the book had been sent to him for review, and he had locked it away so that it should not fall into the hands of anyone else; while one of the most experienced judges of the English law

The Edge of the Abyss

courts, shortly before he died, confided to me the correspondence which had passed between him and the Public Prosecutor with regard to a similar use of the book in England.

Another college professor, in an institution where this poisonous book had been used for the "education" of young boys and girls who were almost unacquainted with the masterpieces of Dante and Milton, or the finer kind of fiction produced in their own country, asked me how I accounted for the fact that Hitler had been suppressing these degenerate books. The fallacious implication, worthy of Lewis Carroll, was that the books ought to be used in schools. There is a far better answer than that. I am entirely against forcible suppression; but, however wicked our enemies in this war may be, they are not fools; and they know perfectly well that a certain way of thought is deadly to the *morale* of any nation. They are quite capable, not only of suppressing it in their own country, therefore, but of fostering it elsewhere. I do not believe that this evil in our midst is native-born; and we have all been behaving like fools about it.

It is not to be forgotten that the book in question came to us under the auspices of Mr. Ezra Pound who for many months has been broadcasting regularly from Rome and pouring abuse upon his own country, the United States, as well as upon England. One of the quite vivid details of this book — which I offer merely as an illustration — primarily concerns English critics. It bespatters the finest memory of their own ruling house, and plasters with ordure the only English sovereign of the nineteenth century who could be praised (or more probably ridiculed) for her goodness. One would have thought that this might have induced a moment's hesitation. I am not offering it as an æsthetic argument. Nor am I a moralist. Poets like Henley and the republican Swinburne were not ashamed to speak well of the sovereign in question; but, if the mood of today is for brutal satire at the expense of simplicity, the mood may be justified by its exponents. That is an entirely different matter from throwing dirt at her — which is exactly what this book did, while two of her children were still living. English critics, above all, should have remembered that, although she was a queen, she was also a woman.

Moreover, if conservative journals — so ready in their literary columns to let anonymous critics sneer at the "vulgarity" of great and enduring modern writers like Kipling — can simultaneously lavish praise on a disgusting alien outrage on their own traditions, on their own memories, their own loyalties, and their own country; if they can thus lick the boots that have trampled on their own national honor — then the abyss certainly opens under everything which their political columns have hitherto pretended to believe in or maintain.

The Edge of the Abyss

Nothing is more false than the familiar suggestion that the book offers us an improvement in literary technique, or indeed anything new. Nothing is older than chaos; and, as for its exploration of the "subconscious," I have dealt with that on another page. But I will add this here. The man who wrote the sleep-walking scene in *Macbeth* concentrated more real knowledge of the subconscious mind into one brief line than the author of *Ulysses* could get into as many pages as there are in the New York telephone book. The man who wrote the opening chapter of *Edwin Drood* knew exactly how to relate the subconscious and the conscious; and when he drew a great anchor up from the depths in *A Tale of Two Cities* he wrote like a master, where the late Mr. Joyce babbled like an idiot. The blind insurrection of the lower faculties, so that they override the conscious mind, indicates merely a pathological condition.

Dr. Jelliffe, clinical professor of mental diseases at Fordham University and visiting neurologist at the City Hospital, New York, quotes some of the scientific authorities on this matter. The amateurs who parade their parrot phrases about "complexes" and "inhibitions" and "frustrations," might do well to read Grasset and pick out a few more novel phrases to impress their readers. I have found that they are usually silenced if one answers them by talking with equal eloquence about "polygonal delirium," which exactly

The Edge of the Abyss

covers the "stream of subconsciousness" in Joyce.

> *Mental confusion* [Grasset says] is a generalized psychosis. Among its peculiarities is a condition of toxic dullness of the superior intellectual activity with a more or less complete domination of it by the subconscious or unconscious dream-activity. [Its delusions are] formed by the fortuitous association of ideas. [The patients] care for nobody. They have only one thought — their own personality.

The author of *Anna Livia Plurabelle* was once told that he made great demands on his readers. "My demand," he replied, "is that my readers should devote their entire lives to the study of my works." This was not a Voltairean joke. He was in deadly earnest. Indeed, a writer in a leading literary journal, after playing the fool by devoting a whole page, including an editorial, to the chaotic cesspool of *Finnegans Wake;* and, solemnly stating that the author was undoubtedly the leader of the most important development in modern fiction, ended his editorial by saying that, unfortunately, in *Finnegans Wake*, the author would have to be content with an audience of one, since he had invented a new language to which nobody else possessed the clue. All this was taken quite seriously by a large section of the intelligentsia. One can be at least glad that the London *Times* declined to print a letter from Mr. T. S. Eliot, in which he placed Mr. Joyce with Milton.

CHAPTER XVI

WE are saved from chaos today, so far as we are saved, merely by what we may call the rules of the traffic, the rules of the road, by conventions that depend for their validity on the very beliefs that we have abandoned. All the pseudo-intelligentsia of modern literature have been engaged in the sublime task of pointing out that even these conventions are worthless; and a vague belief has insidiously been spread by all the machines of publicity throughout the world that the pseudo-intellectuals are right. Wherever there is a straight issue between moral good and moral evil, a large section of the press nearly always describes the latter as "more advanced," not because they really sympathize with it, but because they feel it is more "up to date."

When those conventions, upon which our civilization depends, are put to the test, they are bound to collapse, for, outside the *Civitas Dei*, there is no reality at the present time behind them. They are like a paper currency with nothing, not even credit, in reserve. There is no fundamental belief behind them. Vague talk about ideals is useless. "Ideals," at the present day, may mean anything from polygamy to the total abolition of religion and ethics. No thoughtful and sincere mind looking over Europe today can fail to realize that we are separated from complete chaos by a far thinner barrier than we believed; that the whole fabric of our civilization is being tested by attacks from without and from within and from a thousand directions; and that neither Europe nor America is so secure as we once imagined from the fate of older civilizations.

The chief characteristic of the intellectual world during the last fifty years is its gradual loss of the old simplicity and integrity which went so deep — went right down to the roots of life with men like Milton and Wordsworth in literature, or Abraham Lincoln in statesmanship. This deep integrity of spirit has been replaced everywhere by a shallow cynicism, a spirit of mockery, sometimes clever mockery, but none the less a shining surface with nothing behind it. Mockery and bluff are the characteristics of literature at the present day. It is no exaggeration to say that Matthew Arnold's vague stream of tendency flowing through literature and making for righteousness has been replaced by a stream of tendency which everywhere and on all sides in art and in literature is making for, what again old-fashioned people used to call, wickedness. Despite the occasional good work, and the gleams of beauty that you get here and there, as a kind of afterglow, from the sunset of the great tradition, it is precisely true to say that in the literature of the pseudo-intellectuals we have developed a new and more horrible form of hypocrisy than history has ever known: a hypocrisy which no longer says, "Thank God, I am not as that Publican" but "Thank God, I am not as that Pharisee," for it has made evil its good, and intimidates even the educationalist, who sometimes trembles lest he be accused of righteous judgment.

The inner life of mankind, it was pointed out recently by the Chairman of the British Association at a recent meeting in England, as it has been pointed out by many others, has failed to develop with the extraordinary progress of science. Perhaps as a compensation for the unbounded energy that has been displayed in the physical field, and the profound regard that all true men of science have shown for truth (this regard is one of the very few saving factors in the situation at the present day), there have been signs on every other side of a falling back from the heights that our predecessors had laboriously conquered and a weariness of the effort to maintain them. Sometimes, at its best, this is due to an Epicurean agnosticism which sits as God, "holding no form of creed, but contemplating all." But the world will never solve its problems through mere impartial contemplation of all kinds of belief. Contemplation that can never make up its mind and choose is useless. It is hardly necessary to give examples of the more actively evil kind from the savage brutalities of contemporary art and literature.

There is one hunger which will never be appeased

by bread or circuses. The discontents of the world today are not due to economic causes. They are due to the unsatisfied hunger for the things that belong to our peace in the house not made with hands. In the far simpler conditions of our forefathers the things that belonged to our peace were often found because they had the vision, though distant, of that true and abiding country which was once thought to be the divine pattern of which our earthly best is but a poor symbol and shadow. Our forefathers believed that the soul of man was created for that vision and its ultimate realization. In its possession, though it were only a faint gleam caught from a great way off, there was happiness, because it gave a meaning and a purpose to life. Bereft of it, as the greater part of art and literature testifies today, the human spirit is in torment.

The position is complicated by the fact that this inner loss is very largely due to some of the great achievements of the race. The saying of Hegel that "the divine is the center of all the representations of great art" was essentially true. It corresponded exactly with the statement of Wordsworth about the nature of great poetry and its kinship with religion. Even in pre-Christian days it was certainly true of the Greek drama. The plays of Aeschylus and Sophocles were a form of religious drama. They were profoundly ethical. They were concerned, not with blind fate, as they are so often misrepresented to have been, but with Nemesis — the judgment that overtakes the wrongdoer. They did not preach, though — a little fact that we moderns conveniently forget — the Greek chorus was certainly not afraid of moralizing; but they had a soul and a conscience. This spirit has largely disappeared from our literature, owing to a widespread popular misunderstanding of the results of modern science. Literature and art have never really recovered from the shock of two great scientific discoveries, two great scientific theories. The first was the theory of a certain canon of the Church, Copernicus, which seemed to destroy the old, comfortable assumption that the earth was the center of things, and to dwarf man by the mere size of the material universe. The other was the Darwinian theory, which subjected his inner world to an even more disintegrating scrutiny, and filled mankind with doubts as to the values of human personality and the nature of its origin. But it is not the scientists or the philosophers who are responsible for the troubles from which we are suffering today; it is the pseudo-intellectuals who have followed on their trail. The pseudo-intellectuals have imposed themselves upon a passive world by making impressionable minds accept them and their works at their own valuation. Small clever minds have been exalted into leaders of sects and schools of thought, chiefly on account of their quickness in seizing isolated fragments of truth — fragments that are not even true until they fall into place as parts of an organic whole. In isolation, these fragments may appear to be new and sensational and are, therefore, seized upon by all the machines of publicity, and declared to be as original and valuable as the discovery of the five senses or the seven sins by a new novelist. All too often the reader lacks the intellectual background which would enable him to estimate the value of the fragment in the light of what had already been thought out by uncounted generations before him.

An amusing instance occurs in Mr. H. G. Wells' book, *The Fate of Homo Sapiens* (and it is only one of a thousand in that author's works). He quotes a nursery hymn which he heard in his childhood:

> There's a friend for little children
> Above the bright blue sky

and remarks with a naive contempt that modern astronomy has made that point of view impossible.

Mr. Wells, of course, was blissfully unaware of what Origen had to say about such things nearly two thousand years ago, when that early Father ridiculed the heretic Celsus for supposing that these figures of "up" and "down" or "overhead" entered into the true *philosophia perennis* of Christendom. Celsus, like Mr. Wells, was not concerned with real thought, which has always made a distinction between the material and the spiritual worlds. He was concerned merely to make a debating point which could draw a horselaugh from the crowd; and, for that, a nursery hymn would serve as well as anything else.

There was never a time so chaotic in all its judgments of art and literature, so unable to discriminate between the good and the bad, and so bewildered about all the principles of ethical judgment. There was never a time when our universities so needed to offer up the prayer of the wise king who thought, ages ago, that wisdom did not consist in mathematical knowledge, but in an understanding heart, able to discriminate between good and evil.

Not one of the essentials that belong to our peace has been left to us in its integrity — the religious life has gone, for a great number, and the family, with the affections, is following. In literature the passions are often brutally depicted; but you might read a hundred of the pseudo-moderns and not discover that the ordinary human affections existed at all. It is not the real moderns, it is not the young, but their bewildered elders, who are really responsible. We often hear it said that the young are responsible for the break with tradition and the growing inability to discriminate between the true tradition which is a synonym for development, and the false which is merely static. But just as it was not the young who were responsible for the World War, so it is not the young who are responsible for the post war degradation. It is not the young who have been garlanding the necks of the Muses with festoons of garbage. The young, though their reticence does not always betray the fact, have been robbed of their birthright in Christendom by the jaded cynicism of elderly men of letters, who have been untrue to their intellectual responsibilities. The young come up in each generation with all those shadowy recollections and first affections of which Wordsworth mourned the loss in later life. I think that, sometimes, after they have been subjected to the influences of modern art and literature, they go down from their universities carrying away in their minds nothing that can compensate them for what they have lost, and in the silence and emptiness of their hearts they must often hear a distant echo of that bitterest of all human cries: "They have taken away our Lord . . . and we know not where they have laid Him."

The sense of spiritual values is akin to the intuitions of genius. It cannot be taught, but it can be killed, and nothing can kill it more quickly than the common cynicism, the cynicism of the pseudo-intellectual. Many of the young today may be likened to the young victim of Browning's tragical story:

> I see in the world the intellect of man,
> That sword, the energy his subtle spear,
> The knowledge which defends him like a shield —

The Edge of the Abyss

Everywhere; but they make not up, I think,
The marvel of a soul like thine, earth's flower
She holds up to the softened gaze of God!

Such souls there are daily born into the world; and, though they do not come equipped with what is commonly called knowledge, they do have something before which all other kinds of knowledge seem shallow. Neither Plato nor Wordsworth would dismiss the belief as idle that most souls are endowed with certain powers of direct vision, an inner faculty corresponding to the sight of the physical eyes. Just as the eyes and brain co-operate to make a synthesis of the external world, so do certain spiritual faculties in the young grasp spiritual beauty, apprehend it in a way that sometimes their elders are unable to do. They apprehend spiritual beauty and spiritual truth. It is this process which Plato and Wordsworth described as a kind of remembrance; for what is remembrance, in its literal meaning, but integration — the integration of our world? In this aspect, it is not the peculiar gift of age. It is not merely a looking backward. It is a constructive process dealing with the present reality, and helping us, however brief our past experience may have been, to discover more of that kingdom which transcends time. It belongs especially to youth, and it was for this reason that a greater than Plato or Wordsworth made that sublime appeal in rhythms which seem to speak to us directly from the beating heart of this ordered and rhythmical universe:

> Or ever the silver cord be loosed, or the golden bowl be broken, or the pitcher be broken at the fountain, or the wheel broken at the cistern. Then shall the dust return to the earth as it was: and the spirit shall return unto God who gave it.

Today a great part of our civilization seems to be recapitulating the process which Wordsworth described as taking place in the individual, and to be losing that power of synthesis which is found, at its highest, not in the merely intellectual faculties, but in the vision, sometimes beyond discourse of reason, which was once the common possession of Christendom.

There are signs in the world today that certain leaders in science are beginning to recover that power of synthesis for themselves. I am quite sure that in literature there is no sign of that recovery. We have lost there, in fact, the religion which bound all things in one and gave men a central standard of judgment. There is a common idea that its unifying and central standard of judgment involved an impoverishment of personality; whereas, of course, wherever it really operated it immeasurably enriched human character by enthroning the authority of the universal reason and dethroning blind caprice. The grand old name of the philosophy which formed the intellectual basis of

Christendom, the *philosophia perennis,* was not un-justified. It certainly had a complete answer to the typically "modern" question, "what are you to do about an individual who asserts that for him person-ally our lower values are what he rates most highly?" The appeal in the last resort must be to reason, which does not depend on caprice, but on universal principles. It dethrones caprice and enthrones the Logos.

. It is thus, and only thus, that we can reconcile the two necessary principles of Freedom and Authority and save the world from the greatest tyranny that the world has ever known, the tyranny of fashion, the tyranny of "the contemporary mind," the tyranny that forces men to walk in processions and believe they are being original, the tyranny which makes us intel-lectually subservient to the dictatorships of an hour.

Justifiably enough for his own purposes, the analyti-cal specialist in every department of thought today has been leading the world along a diminishing road, a road that eventually runs out into nothingness, if ultimate explanations are sought in that direction.

Science has accomplished marvels for the material comfort of mankind along just those lines which Macaulay praised Sir Francis Bacon for laying down. They were not, of course, the invention of Bacon, though Macaulay in one ludicrous sentence actually compared the beneficence of Bacon with that of the Author of the Universe. In the popular mind, and in literature, scientific methods have been divorced from philosophy, and a widespread belief has arisen in direct defiance of the first axioms of science, that the greater values can be produced by the less. Popular theories of evolution (I distinguish between the popular and the more philosophical theories, of course) are of the kind that would account for a Beethoven symphony by attributing it to the catgut in the violins and then tracing the pedigree of the cat. Every step of the process would be accurate, exquisitely accurate, as far as it goes; the only trouble is that it omits the most important factors in the problem: the musical values of the symphony itself; and, most essential of all, its creator, the composer.

Mr. Julian Huxley told us a little time ago that the idea of a personal God was born in the mind of man. But that is hardly a valid objection from a man who wishes us to accept his own ideas. The idea was the result of a reasoning process — a process which, as we have seen, transcends all personal predilections, and is universally valid, having a certain relationship even to the Eternal Logos. It was aided by those intuitions and that faculty in us which goes as deep and is as mysterious as life itself. To turn the tables on Mr. Huxley, I wonder where the idea of a mechanical universe was born. We are told to beware of anthropomorphism. We are warned that we must not look for explanations in terms of the highest that we know, or we may be led astray. But what about explanations couched in even more inadequate terms? The idea of a mechanical universe, of course, is based on a comparison of the universe with the man-made machines of which we have actual experience. But all of these illustrative machines are made by intelligence, directed by intelligence, and used for a purpose. The people who talk about a mechanical universe usually omit just those three important characteristics of all these illustrative machines: that they are made by intelligence, directed by intelligence, and used for a purpose. They are comparing the universe, therefore, with something that does not exist, a monstrous chimera.

Moreover, they are eliminating the idea of Freedom, which emerges at a certain level of evolution as "free will," and depends also upon "reason," which — as was said above — delivers us from the bondage both of mechanical processes and of caprice, and is the ground of reconciliation between Freedom and Authority in the life of the Spirit. All this complex and highly organized humanistic and religious structure, however, is ignored or shattered by the sheer incompetence of a great body of recent thought.

We can hardly overestimate the harm that has been done to the modern world in the destruction of all its highest values by the foolish "intellectual" war that was proclaimed in the early days of the Darwinian theory between science and religion. The vague popular idea that religion and theism are out of date and Christianity an idle dream is, of course, directly trace-able to it; and so also are many of the new brutalities in art, literature and psychology. Justified as "realism," these manifestations are directly connected with what is now called "real politics," though it used to be called "crime." There is not and there never was any ground for such a war between science and religion. There is not any ground for attempting to reconcile them in any premature way. The scientific statement that there is a skeleton under the skin of a living man is not neces-sarily inconsistent with that man's portrait by an artist, or with his personal character as it appears to his friends and those who love him. If either side had fully under-stood the other, they would have been in agreement.

Darwin's theory of evolution, for instance, in almost all its alleged facts — as distinguished from explana-tions — seems to be true as far as it goes. But for litera-ture, and the mind of the world as we know it today, and the minds of the younger generation at the univer-sities, it has been made to mean something that no real thinker could accept for a moment. At one end of the process it is supposed we have a nebula, a cloud of gas drifting about in space; and out of the action and re-action of the chemical elements in that cloud of gas, and nothing else whatsoever, the human race has slowly and surely emerged, with Beethoven and Shakespeare, and the great cathedrals, and London and New York, and all that they imply. Or you can begin at a later stage, if you like. You can begin at the time when this planet was absolutely lifeless (as the scientists assure us it once was). You can imagine yourself coming as an immortal agnostic from another planet and sitting down alone on the shores of a lifeless sea, confident that, if you waited there in patience for a sufficient length of time, the chemical processes of that lifeless earth and sea one sure and certain day would initiate a series of events whereby the *Mauretania* would go sailing past you, and a little boy would run up to you and offer you *The New York Times*. But if you can imagine a confidence so sublime I can only suggest that the faith of the agnostic in physical processes is far greater than has yet been realized.

The textbooks have confused the issue by concentrating attention on masses of detail between those stages; and in the popular press, in literature today, and in the minds of many young students at the universities, evolution really means just that monstrous method of obtaining plus out of minus. Well might Darwin write words which both his enemies and his friends have forgotten to read:

> That grand sequence of events which our minds refuse to accept as the result of blind chance. The understanding [he wrote in *The Descent of Man*] revolts at such a conclusion.

153

The Edge of the Abyss

It was the strongest language that Darwin ever used. Why has it been completely forgotten? Why has this revolt of Darwin been forgotten in that modern revolt of which we hear so much from the popular press — the "revolt" which has made a great part of modern literature so revolting? Did they think he was lying when he said it — the most emphatic sentence he ever uttered, and couched in the most noble language he ever used? Why have they swept it so completely aside that it is never mentioned even in a whisper? It is perfectly obvious to what other conclusion Darwin was quite definitely pointing in that sentence, although he refused as a man of science to go any further in his speculations in that direction. He said once (you will find it in his biography), that he didn't wish to speculate on those subjects because it seemed to him that the mind of the Creator must be as far above the mind of man as the mind of Newton was above that of a dog.

It was not a very accurate or a very strong way of stating the real truth. It has been much better stated in a much older way: "As the heavens are higher than the earth, so are my thoughts higher than your thoughts." The distance between the mind of Newton and the dog is measurable; the other distance is immeasurable.

It is unfortunate that the opposite conclusion, the negative conclusion, against which Darwin revolted so strongly, has been accepted by the greater part of the less thoughtful public today as Darwin's chief contribution to science. We have been taught by the very moderns who reject the miraculous in every direction, that this miracle has taken place, that plus has been produced out of minus; that this gigantic organized universe of ours has emerged out of a homogeneous and lifeless gas, and that this has happened without the movement of any higher Power working through, directing, and inspiring the process.

It should be possible somehow in our universities — literature at one time I thought could do it, but I don't think so now — to devise some means of enabling the student to focus his mind differently, according to the different orders of truth that he is considering.

Science tells us that all matter is composed of infinitesimal planetary systems of electrons and protons. Magnify in imagination a certain small part of the material world, the human countenance you love best. Magnify it through a microscope of inconceivable size until you can see it (with your mind's eye, at any rate) as a sort of Milky Way of such infinitesimal electrical systems. You may have been following quite accurately one order of truth, you may have arrived quite accurately at one order of truth, but what has happened to the values in the human countenance that you loved best? What has become of the expression in the eyes? What has become of the human affections that shone through them? Where do they reside? Is it somewhere in the interstellar spaces, as they may be called, between those electrical units? Or is it in the electrical units themselves? Isn't it possible that science in giving us its details has somehow made us lose sight of the chief values in the universe? Isn't it possible that it has somehow lost the real significance, and that the real significance may be more apparent to the child whose eyes are normally focused, not on electrons, but on the affection expressed in the countenance they love best. If so this is only one more confirmation from a new angle, of a very old statement about philosophers and children.

In all the results of science today we are witnessing an extraordinary, though largely unconscious, corroboration of the essentials of the greatest idealistic philosophy, the closest approximation to ultimate spiritual truth that the world has ever known, the *philosophia perennis* of Christendom. I don't want to particularize any more than that. Neither side is yet fully aware of this corroboration, for neither side, perhaps, has yet learned the necessity of adjusting the focus of its eyes to the order of truth that it is contemplating. "Nature red in tooth and claw" is not essentially different from the creation that St. Paul saw groaning and travailing together, with Calvary as its consummate centre, except that St. Paul was seeing it in its ultimate aspect, relating it to its ultimate origin, and therefore went deeper and was nearer to the ultimate spiritual truth about it. Science, again, is daily demonstrating the power of the mind to master the laws of nature and gain control of its material environment. As the mind grows, the control grows. We can assign no limits to the process, even on this planet. To say the very least of it, this is not inconsistent with the profoundest belief of religion, that the supreme control, if there *be* any supreme control, is vested in Supreme Mind.

To seek the explanation of the lower in the higher, rather than of the higher in the lower, is not, after all, illogical; and it leads directly to the belief that the explanation of the whole is to be found only in the Highest. There is a harmony in things which makes it possible for flashes of intuition to illuminate regions that are quite impenetrable to the ploddings of inductive logic. "The glory of the sum of things" is too vast and too complex for logic to survey even one cloud thread in its first elementary fringes. But the glory of that infinite harmony can flash along the chords of the mind in great fleeting moments, when the mind lives at the centre with Plato and St. John and ceases to wander along the infinitely distant circumference with its electric torches. The Supreme Mind may be as far above our human conception of intellectual processes as the immediate apprehension of Love is above the processes of logic. There can be no "discourse" of reason in it, moving from point to point, but only universal Light, that Light "whose smile kindles the universe," even as it is its Wisdom and its Spirit. But it is above "discourse," not below it.

> The reality of an ordered world [says the late Dr. Charles Gore] can exist only for mind and in terms of mind. There seems to be no way of escaping this conclusion. The real world of a fly or a dog — whatever it may be — requires the mind of a fly or a dog for its existence. There is a co-operation in the matter. The Man's world of fuller reality requires the man's mind. The whole of the world-reality in all its fullness and complexity postulates a universal and perfect mind which (whether it is to be represented as its Creator or as its Soul) would be instinctively called divine, and it is this divine mind which is communicating with us through all the process of sensitive experience in art and in literature. In knowing more about the world, I am learning about God.

CHAPTER XVII

Iᴛ is precisely in this that the true end of human life is found. At a certain stage in evolution, man did rise to the apprehension of a higher spiritual life, in which the circle of Infinity was rounded, and he could meet and communicate with the Eternal Power that made him. It is the central doctrine of Christianity that this Eternal Power, being the Origin and End of all things, and the permanent Ground, subsisting through all changes, must influence and affect every event, every act, every atom of the universe, and that it did actually at a certain stage in human development, "stoop to man that man might rise to God." It is precisely in this increasing knowledge and expanding vision that the purpose and happiness of human life are fulfilled. It is precisely this that made the value of the individual soul, upon which alone the true theory of democracy is based. It was not on "anthropomorphic" grounds, but because the spirit of man could apprehend (though it might not comprehend) the eternal values, that it was said to be made in the image of God.

As Mr. Walter Lippmann wrote recently, in a striking essay on "education without culture":

The institutions of the Western world were formed by men who learned to regard themselves as inviolable persons because they were rational and free. They meant by 'rational' that they were capable of comprehending the moral order of the universe and their place in this moral order. . . .

Yet the historic fact is that the institutions we cherish — and now know we must defend against the most determined and efficient attack ever organized against them — are the products of a culture which, as Gilson put it, "is essentially the culture of Greece, inherited from the Greeks by the Romans, transfused by the Fathers of the Church with the religious teachings of Christianity, and progressively enlarged by countless numbers of artists, writers, scientists and philosophers from the beginning of the Middle Ages up to the first third of the nineteenth century."

Modern education, however, is based on a denial that it is necessary or useful or desirable for the schools and colleges to transmit from generation to generation the religious and classical culture of the Western world.

He remarks that education as a direct result of this has become merely "careerist." There is no common faith, no common body of knowledge, no common moral and intellectual discipline; and there is a direct connection between this, and the demonstrable collapse of reason, the demonstrable weakening of the power to think soundly in our time; while, "in the fierce struggle for existence, they are tearing Western society to pieces."

The Edge of the Abyss

By separating education from the classical religious tradition [says Mr. Lippmann] the school cannot train the pupil to look upon himself as an inviolable person because he is made in the image of God. These very words, though they are the noblest words in our language, now sound archaic.

And yet, as I said earlier, it is just in this last belief that we find the only possible ground of reconciliation between freedom and authority, the inviolable rights of the individual and his duties to his fellow man. Bereft of it, nobody can "look upon society" as a brotherhood arising out of a conviction that men are made in a common image.

It is by this conception of brotherhood; and, at its highest, membership in the mystical Body of Christ, that our liberty is so gloriously bound. As a profoundly true article in *The Commonweal* said recently:

Our glorious liberty bids a man to keep his word whether to his wife or his neighbor, not because someone has decided that would be a good plan, but because as a child of God he is dealing with God's children in God's way.

The same writer, however, gives a warning which — as instances given earlier may illustrate — is particularly cogent at this moment. He speaks of the attempt "to use Christianity as a means to other ends."

The Edge of the Abyss

It can be detected in the unqualified identifying of Christianity with the anti-totalitarian powers, and the zeal of certain politicians, themselves not professed or practicing Christians, to emphasize the irreligiousness of totalitarianism.

Christendom cannot be reconstituted to save the European tradition and culture, but a recovered Christian faith would breathe new life into Europe.

One of the commonest fallacies of this hour is the statement that Christianity has failed. As Chesterton once answered, "It cannot have failed. It has never been tried." The failure of human beings to live up to it; their failure in their misunderstandings and false interpretations of it, cannot be attributed to religion.

One thing is quite certain — that the most elementary attempts to live up to it, if they were really sincere, would make it impossible for the individuals concerned to emulate the wickedness that prevails today in so many high places.

The problem deeply concerns the educationalist. In literature today, especially in the literature of the English-speaking peoples, we have the most powerful means of communicating thought that the world has ever known. Literature and art, moreover, should have a very important function in saving the student from the dangers of specialism, and enabling him to reintegrate his world after the specialist has dissected it. It should provide him with a world of golden logic, in tune with the universal harmonies; a world where the horse is no longer drawn by the cart; a world where the higher values that seem to come last in the order of nature take their proper place and — as the great Greek philosopher said — "come first in the order of thought." This is the true realm of the mind; a realm in which the spirit begins to see all things in one, by direct vision, with Thomas à Kempis; a realm in which the things that are seen become a kind of parable of the things that are unseen. It holds nothing in common with superstition; for it is too full of the one miraculous reality, and knows that the whole universe and everything in it is a miracle, transcending reason, defying comprehension, and resting ultimately on that Being, beyond all our contingent shadow-shows, which required no other to produce it, and is sufficient to itself, and in the *philosophia perennis* of Christendom is called *God*.

This metaphysical basis of everything that exists is the prime Fact of which, as Herbert Spencer, the leading agnostic philosopher of the last century, declared in his great chapter on the Unknowable, we are more certain than of anything else whatsoever. "Unknowable" he called it; but so did St. John, in the opening chapter of the Fourth Gospel; and, as Spencer went on to say, our reason forced us to endow this ultimate and perennial Reality with certain attributes, and in these postulates the philosophy of science was at one with the philosophy of religion. We know, for instance, that it is the ultimate origin of all things: the starry heavens above us and the moral law within; the material universe and the works of Shakespeare and Beethoven. We know that it is the permanent ground of the whole process of what we call "evolution," the inscrutable Factor which enables us to account for the apparent emergence of plus out of minus, the higher values out of the lower. And since it has no Cause beyond itself, but is the permanent ground of all things, it transcends the world of "nature" in which everything is caused by something else. Therefore, Spencer described it not only as Unknowable, but "perfect, infinite and *supernatural*." And, in all this, he is reaffirming, as he says, the primary postulate of both Science and Religion.

In other words, the leading agnostic of the last century at least affirmed that the most important and most certain Factor in every act and atom of the universe was that ultimate Being which could only be described as "supernatural." The word "supernatural," by misuse, has acquired superstitious connotations; and it may be preferable for present purposes to say that the *metaphysical* basis of the world of thought is a demonstrable fact. It has been obscured only by the bewildering flood of modern specialisms whose exponents can only achieve their immediate results by ignoring fundamental questions. As Lotze remarked, a ship's captain, steering through dangerous waters, has no time to discuss the freedom of the will. But this does not dispossess him; nor does it invalidate the great saying of Goethe that "in ultimates we see God."

It is a significant fact that the most vital thinking now being done in England and America is a development from Aquinas. Nobody could have been more severely critical of the abuses of Catholicism than Dean Inge, our greatest living Platonist; yet, both in conversation and in writing, he has told me that he has found more intellectual sustenance in the neo-Thomists (including Maritain in France), than in any other writers. In America, there has been nothing of late quite so vital as some of the writings and addresses of Dr. Mortimer J. Adler of Chicago University.

> The modern culture [says Dr. Adler] will be achieved only when all the goodness of science can be praised without losing any of the goodness in philosophy and religion, only when the truths of philosophy and religion can be integrally retained without losing any of the true advances in knowledge.

It is an educational specialism that chiefly stands in the way of this reintegration; but, as I tried to show in another book, *The Unknown God*, the task of re-integration (which is certainly possible for individuals) ought not to be beyond the capacity of contemporary thought as a whole. But Dr. Adler lays his finger on one great obstacle in many thinkers of our time. They are not co-operatively seeking for an agreement about the truth. They are not seeking for the ground on which Spencer and Kant and Aquinas, despite the differences of terminology, might be seen to be adumbrating the same truth. They are chiefly anxious to show how they themselves differ from every possible predecessor, under the mistaken impression that this will confirm their own "originality."

It seems likely that, if some real truth-seeker were to arrive at a genuine synthesis of what his predecessors had achieved, and that the hope of reintegrating our modern world depended on the recognition of its truth, it would be immediately followed by a flood of illogical and even nonsensical "originalities" obscuring the whole issue and designed merely to advertise themselves.

This spirit, as Dr. Adler says, "justifies the most extreme pessimism about an impending catastrophe. The Tower of Babel we are building invites another flood."

The modern, "beyond the field of science, cannot be instructed because he acknowledges no ignorance. Hence anyone who would try to instruct him about philosophical or religious truths would be regarded as authoritarian, as trying to impose a doctrine. . . . Even though such truth can be attained only by the free activity of each mind, the fact that *no mind is free to reject the truth* seems like an infringement of his sacred liberties. . . . On fundamental questions, which means all the questions beyond the scope of science, he wishes to keep a thoroughly open mind for ever; he wishes neither to be convinced of anything nor to convince anyone."

But the questions which have brought us to the edge of the abyss are precisely those fundamental questions of good and evil, right and wrong, and the existence of a Power above the State, which are beyond the scope of science, though the wisdom of the ages can most certainly deliver answers to them.

In my former book, *The Unknown God*, to which I have referred, I attempted to restate and give reasons for those answers, which may be briefly summarized here:

1. That there is a great "consilience of inductions," as well as an immense mass of evidence derived from the inner life and experience of the human race, which constitute an overwhelming proof of the first postulate of reason, and of a rightly ordered society, namely, belief in the existence of a Supreme Being, our Origin and End, from whose very nature the imperatives of conscience and the distinction between right and wrong, good and evil, justice and injustice, are derived.

2. That it is in the realm of spiritual values, not in the quantitative measurements of the material world, that we approach most nearly to a realization of the nature of that Supreme Being. The nature of the divine, the nature of God, in other words, is revealed to us in the inner life of the individual personal soul, which is not susceptible of any physical measurements, rather than in any aspects of the material world, the rocks and stones and trees in which the Pantheist would find it. A child, with its possibilities of love and aspiration towards God, is therefore not only more valuable than any quantity of lifeless matter, but is — despite Copernicus — more central and *nearer* to God.

3. It is therefore not irrational, but in conformity with the highest reason, to look for the fullest revelation of the character of God, the Supreme Being, where we come nearest to finding it (i. e., in the conscious human soul, with its divine possibilities of love and sacrifice, and its intellectual grasp of things beyond the reach of the senses).

4. That the central belief of the Christian religion, in completely rational conformity with this, is that the Light has thus shone in our darkness, though the darkness cannot comprehend it; that man, in the course of evolution, has reached a point where it is possible for him to meet, touch,

and communicate with the divine and the realities of a higher world than that of the beasts; and that the character of God has been most nearly and profoundly revealed to us in the most divine of all human and divine characters, approaching us in history (not through the vague mists of endless time or a boundless physical universe) and saying, as none other could say, "I am the Resurrection and the Life."

5. That the world-wide attack on the religion founded by Christ has been based on a complete misunderstanding of the relation between the measurements of science, in the phenomenal world, and the spiritual values which belong to the world of ultimate Reality; that this misunderstanding has been fostered and spread by incompetent thinkers, inadequately acquainted with the great results of human thought in the past.

6. That the present conflict can only be won in the realms of thought, by rediscovering the rational and basic principles of our religion. (It calls for a great counterattack, by competent thinkers, on the whole evil brood of false materialistic sophistries. There is an overwhelming body of truth in the intellectual armories of Christendom which has only to be rightly used to ensure a change of heart and mind throughout the world.)

7. That in this way, and in this way alone, the

values of the individual souls, upon which the true theory of democracy depends, can rationally be asserted, together with the true aims of human life, here and in Eternity.

8. That the State thus must subserve each and every individual, while the duty of the individual to the State is based upon membership in a Body transcending all national groups. It is only in the Fatherhood of God, the Power above the State, that the brotherhood of man can be rationally asserted, and his individual and inalienable rights reconciled with his duties towards any earthly State. It is this and this alone that can complete the circle, and establish a basis upon which States (otherwise unfettered in their aims) can live in harmony with one another and make just claims upon the individuals composing them. Bereft of this, democracy itself becomes a corrupt system of bribery, wherein the power-greedy bribe the electorate by offering them the goods of others in return for their votes. Internationally, this again means war.

9. That only in this restoration of the basic religious principles of Christendom, can Art, Literature and the processes of the human reason be rescued from the chaos into which they have been collapsing, and reestablished on their primary foundations, with true standards of judgment

and all their values in hierarchical order, proportion and harmony.

10. That this restoration depends very largely on a change in the spirit of our education, which has been too exclusively secular and "careerist."

11. Since it is true that this material universe has become a vehicle of spiritual values — "the Word made Flesh" — a new significance is given to the great statement of Goethe on the sacramental nature of the Christian religion.

Goethe's description of how human life is bound together from birth to the grave by the sacraments of religion is one of the few really constructive passages in his autobiography. It can be best summed up in one of the oldest and noblest prayers of Christendom, a prayer which is not only in perfect accord with the theories of evolution but brings out their deeper possibilities of significance by relating them to that Eternal Origin and End which must also be a permanent Factor in every act, event and atom of the universe:

God, who in a wonderful manner hast created and ennobled human nature, and still more wonderfully renewed it, grant that through these sacramental elements we may be made partakers of His divinity, who vouchsafed to become partaker of our humanity.

The Edge of the Abyss

It is only as members of this mystical Body, the *Civitas Dei*, that we can reintegrate the life of the world, or rediscover the unity, the hope and the true end of human life. Outside that City, as a great writer said recently, there is only the Night.

THE END